Equality in an Unequal World

EQUALITY IN AN UNEQUAL WORLD

A Convoco Edition

CORINNE MICHAELA FLICK (ED.)

Convoco! Editions

The publisher has used its best endeavors to ensure that the URLs for
external websites referred to in this book are correct and active at the
time of going to press. However, the publisher has no responsibility for
the websites and can make no guarantee that a site will remain live or
that the content is or will remain appropriate.

Convoco Foundation
Brienner Strasse 28
D – 80333 Munich
www.convoco.co.uk

British Library Cataloguing-in-Publication data: a catalogue
record for this book is available from the British Library.

Edited by Dr. Corinne Michaela Flick
Translated from German by Philippa Hurd
Layout and typesetting by Jill Sawyer Phypers
Printed and bound in Great Britain by Clays Ltd., St Ives plc

ISBN: 978-1-9163673-6-4

Previously published Convoco titles:

How much Freedom must we Forgo to be Free? (2022)

**New Global Alliances: Institutions, Alignments and Legitimacy in the
Contemporary World (2021)**

The Standing of Europe in the New Imperial World Order (2020)

The Multiple Futures of Capitalism (2019)

The Common Good in the 21st Century (2018)

Authority in Transformation (2017)

Power and its Paradoxes (2016)

To Do or Not To Do—Inaction as a Form of Action (2015)

Dealing with Downturns: Strategies in Uncertain Times (2014)

Collective Law-Breaking—A Threat to Liberty (2013)

Who Owns the World's Knowledge? (2012)

**Can't Pay, Won't Pay? Sovereign Debt and the Challenge of Growth in
Europe (2011)**

Respect for humanity! Respect for humanity! If such respect is rooted in the human heart, humanity will eventually establish a social, political, or economic system that reflects it.

Antoine de Saint-Exupéry (1900–1944)

CONTENTS

Introduction   1

Theses   7

1. What is the Optimal Level   15
   of Inequality?
   Francisco H. G. Ferreira

2. Distributive and Social Equality   39
   Jonathan Wolff

3. Equality in the Law   55
   Marietta Auer

4. Equality in an Unequal World: 75
   Historical Perspectives
   Jörn Leonhard

5. Justice or Just Is? Economics and   89
    Inequality
    Raji Jayaraman

6. Romantic Love and   103
    Intergenerational Mobility
    Kai A. Konrad

7. Social Mobility and Meritocracy   113
    Clemens Fuest

8. Reversing Polarization: How People   127
    can find Common Purpose
    Paul Collier

9. Guaranteed Prosperity?   141
    The German Experience
    Wolfgang Schön

10. Democratic Equality and Changes in   151
    Modern Liberal Democracies
    Claudia Wiesner

11. The World After Empire: on the Role   173
    of Trade in Efforts at Making the
    World More Equal
    Mathias Risse

12. A New Era of Trade Policy   193
    and Power Politics
    Gabriel Felbermayr

13. Equality, Inequality, Law   217
    Christoph G. Paulus

14. Equality—From Postulate to Problems   233
    Stefan Korioth

15. Leadership in the Anthropocene—   247
    Recognizing and Counteracting Inequalities
    in Relation to the Natural World
    Timo Meynhardt

16. Architecture for a Global Community   273
    Francis Kéré & Hans Ulrich Obrist
    in Conversation

    Contributors   287

    Podcast Conversations   305

INTRODUCTION

Dear Friends of Convoco,

Inequality—like the related qualities of difference and otherness—is a basic characteristic of being human. Everything that exists does so in a relation of difference. Conversely, it's not easy to talk about equality. There are many kinds and manifestations of equality: political, legal, economic, social, and—fundamentally—the moral equality of human beings, which goes back to the need to be the author of one's own life. The forms of equality to which various groups aspire are various: equality under the law, equality of distribution (everyone having the same power, resources, and chances in education), and finally equality of opportunities and basic conditions. That was and still is the goal that perhaps most strive for. But it is a long way from being achieved, and there are many who argue that it is likely to prove as unattainable as many of equality's other forms.

The question arises as to whether there can be equality between people, or whether it can be created. And if so, what kind of equality is sought? History has shown that *complete equality*, i.e., identity between people is impossible to achieve. Complete equality is probably also undesirable given the ever more prominent movements created around "identity politics." Individuality means emphasizing what is special and particular about a person, and thus distinguishing oneself and indeed not being the *same*. Thus, at least at first glance, identity and equality are mutually contradictory.

As a result, we must redefine equality and conceive of it differently. What does equality mean if there cannot be equality on an individual level? Following Aristotle, this means treating equals equally and unequals unequally. Every person should be treated equally unless they are different in relevant ways. This principle must be the starting point when it comes to establishing rules and systems in a society in order to allow the possibility of justice.

The fight for equality, the struggle to achieve equality, has a checkered history of highs and lows, because the starting point of the pursuit of equality is always inequality. There are many manifestations of inequality, and every country has a different form of inequality. Even in Western Europe, inequality varies between individual countries. It is almost impossible to talk about equality in general. What is certain, however, is that without a high level of social equality, the ideal of the common good will be lost. And there is broad agreement that the common good forms the basis of a healthy society.

Since the end of the 18th century there has been a momentous, and at times highly destructive, drive towards more and more equality. This path has led through revolutions, two World Wars (wars are always periods when differences are leveled out while simultaneously being their catalyst),[1] via such movements as the founding of trade unions and the admission of women to political and educational rights, through to the more recent struggles for civil rights and to today's movements such as MeToo and Black Lives Matter.

This brings us to the identity-politics movements of recent years. And this is where we must recognize that identity means distinguishing oneself and not being the same. The goal is therefore equality of unequals. In this spirit, the theme of this book is *Equality in an Unequal World*.

We should recognize that equality between individuals exists only in ignorance, powerlessness, and inability to control. We are all equally helpless in the face of major problems and challenges. This is an equality deriving from impotence and not from power, as the thinker Bazon Brock explains. Global challenges such as climate change give rise to global equality: even if we are all affected unequally, we as individuals are all equally powerless in the face of such problems. Not even a new global divide, which is becoming apparent as a result of the war in Ukraine, will change that. The global equality outlined above still pertains, even in a world divided between liberal democracies and autocracies. We should not lose sight of this point when we talk about equality.

Thus, equality should not be defined at the level of the individual, but at the macroeconomic level in our systems, by treating equals equally and unequals unequally. It is also important to note what the philosopher Tim Crane has emphasized in his recent Convoco podcast: equality in relation to human dignity. Equal dignity must be accorded to every person and every social group: "People are born equal in the sense that everyone is deserving of the same basic respect—this is the core idea behind equality."[2]

The principle of equal opportunities has thus far been considered the most efficient and appropriate means of creating equality. It applies at the point of departure. But even here questions arise. Equal opportunities are not sufficient to create a just and diverse world, and according to the latest neuroscientific findings it is also a completely inadequate starting point.[3] It is impossible to give people the same point of departure, because upbringing in early childhood plays an essential role in an individual's development. The extent to which a mother takes care of her baby or toddler can only be marginally influenced by the state or society. However, any subsequent compensation to ensure a fair and equitable outcome remains an unsatisfactory means of correcting a dysfunctional equality of opportunity.

Today we have reached a new point of development as far as the issue of equality is concerned. The need to establish compensatory measures at macroeconomic level applies to countries and continents too. Equality despite, and precisely because of, inequality has now become a crucial issue. Global threats demand more equality because they create new inequalities. Pandemics, climate change, and the resulting migration will make changes inevitable. History has taught us that it is better to embrace change, thereby controlling it to some degree, than to resist it. In our own interest, we are all called upon to create more equality. The goal must be a fairer world.

Corinne Michaela Flick, January 2023

Notes

1. Jörn Leonhard, "Equality in an Unequal World: Historical Perspectives" in the present volume, pp. 75–88.

2. Tim Crane and Corinne Flick, "Why Equality is about Dignity and Respect," CONVOCO! Podcast #80, July 2022.

3. Francisco H. G. Ferreira, "What is the Optimal Level of Inequality?" in the present volume, pp. 24–25.

THESES

CORINNE MICHAELA FLICK

We should treat equals equally and unequals unequally. This principle must be the starting point when it comes to establishing rules and systems in a society in order to allow the possibility of justice. Equality should not be defined at the level of the individual, but at the macroeconomic level in our systems, because individuality means distinguishing oneself and indeed not being the same.

FRANCISCO H. G. FERREIRA

"What is the optimal level of inequality?" is a complex normative question, inextricably related to our broad conception of social justice. If it were possible to preserve all freedoms, increase prosperity, and eliminate all income differences at the same time, then "zero" might be the answer for the income space. But that is an impossible task.

JONATHAN WOLFF

Equality of opportunity is competitive and often requires us to have humiliating capacity testing for the people we're trying to help. Therefore, we should think differently about equality. Equality is really about respect for everyone rather than the distribution of things.

MARIETTA AUER

Equality has been one of the law's most important concerns since antiquity. Nevertheless, the law cannot fulfil every conceivable claim to equality. A central concern of justice in the law is the creation of formal equality between persons. Legal measures that aim to establish substantive equality beyond that must be balanced against countervailing civil liberties on a case-by-case basis.

JÖRN LEONHARD

A strained relationship between promises of equality and experiences of inequality characterized many social developments since the 19th century. It influenced the credibility of laws, regimes, and actors—and continues to do so today.

RAJI JAYARAMAN

Economics has an indispensable set of empirical tools to understand and address inequality. But unless applied economists find a way to incorporate justice into their otherwise remarkable toolkit, they risk losing their relevance in the eyes of a public hungry for justice.

KAI A. KONRAD

Anyone whose primary goal is striving for more equality of wealth would have to entertain the idea of declaring war on the institutions that promote endogamy, that is class-conscious marriage.

CLEMENS FUEST

A temporary decrease in social mobility may arise as part of a normal process of development as societies shift towards more meritocratic structures with wider opportunities for advancement.

PAUL COLLIER

European leadership will need people with the moral decency to bring people together around a socially worthwhile purpose. They will need the communication skills to set that purpose as a common goal. And they will need the modesty to devolve agency to others.

WOLFGANG SCHÖN

The COVID-19 pandemic and the energy crisis have drawn the state increasingly into the role of guaranteeing existing prosperity. Politicians consider it their duty to protect citizens from all kinds of turns of fate and not just guarantee a minimum social level. This policy often results merely in greater redistribution. The goal must be to equip society and the economy as a whole with resilience to face external influences.

CLAUDIA WIESNER

The preconditions and contexts of liberal democracy are changing: digitalization changes democratic practices, experts gain influence, and the room for decision-making in national democracies in a globalized world is reduced. These changes affect democracy and endanger the principle of democratic equality.

MATHIAS RISSE

We must never stop thinking about how we are implementing trade in an international and domestic system so that internationally countries are treated in some way approximating a status as equal participants in an international trade regime.

GABRIEL FELBERMAYR

Protectionism is not a suitable means of combating inequality. Much more effective and efficient instruments are available for this purpose. Yet such instruments must actually be implemented so that the advantages of the international division of labor reach as many people as possible.

CHRISTOPH G. PAULUS

The law has always tried to create equality—not on a comprehensive basis, of course, but often only with regard to a small group. As an instrument for creating equality, however, it will always be necessary.

STEFAN KORIOTH

Equality of outcome is the challenge of today. Making this a central issue reduces the freedom to act to the possibilities that remain once equality has been established.

TIMO MEYNHARDT

It is not enough if people see themselves as part of nature but attribute a separate value to it. The crucial step is the recognition of nature's agency. Only then can inequalities in relation to nature be suitably addressed.

HANS ULRICH OBRIST

Francis Kéré's work seeks to encourage those who have not been given the opportunity to fulfil their potential—quite literally building spaces for equality in an unequal world. His Serpentine Pavilion 2017 sought to connect its visitors to nature and to each other, speaking to the importance of equality among all living beings.

FRANCIS KÉRÉ

The buildings inherited from the colonial past were built with high walls to protect decision-makers and their fake political system. I want my public buildings to be open gathering spaces. They should be walkable and accessible at any time. In this way, I hope political leaders will be forced to make the right decisions.

CHAPTER 1

WHAT IS THE OPTIMAL LEVEL OF INEQUALITY?

FRANCISCO H. G. FERREIRA

Is there an optimal level of inequality?[1] This question may be provocative. How should we think about what we want? What kind of society should we desire and seek to promote in terms of the distributional question?

Let's start with the basic fact that the extent of income inequality varies a very great deal in the world. The World Bank's *Poverty and Shared Prosperity Report* documents trends in inequality between and within countries around the world.[2] It provides estimates of income inequality for a large number of countries in

2013 using a common measure of inequality, the Gini coefficient, which is an index that takes the value zero if everybody has the same income and a hundred if just one person has all the income.[3] The level of inequality in the world ranges from around 24 in some of the most equal countries, including for example Slovenia and Norway, to above 50 in the most unequal ones, which include countries like my own, Brazil, as well as Colombia, Honduras, Haiti, and South Africa (the most unequal with a Gini of 63.4 in 2013).

Given this wide array of levels of inequality, the question is if there is an optimal level. One might say the optimal level is zero, because there should not be any inequality. However, inequality is not the only thing we care about. We are also interested in what can be described as growth. We pay attention to factors that have nothing to do with income or wealth such as people's rights and freedoms. If it were possible to preserve all freedoms, maintain a very dynamic economy based on growth, and reduce inequality to zero at the same time, then we would do that. But that is an impossible task. The question "What is the optimal level of inequality?" is complicated because it is a normative question of social justice, of what makes a good society. This goes back to Aristotle: what we want from a society will have an overwhelming bearing on the question of what the distribution should look like. What the optimal level of inequality is cannot be answered independently of our views of what makes a fair society.

To answer this question, I would like to briefly review four important perspectives that have been dominant in the recent history of political philosophy: utilitarianism, libertarianism, Amartya Sen's Capability Approach, and a theory of equality of opportunity. In doing so, I want to discuss each theory's "basal space," which may be understood as the variables that matter for the assessment of justice, and how each theory aggregates information about that basal space over individuals.

Utilitarianism has a long history going back to Jeremy Bentham at University College London at the end of the 18th century. Amartya Sen has described utilitarianism as very pervasive and having a tremendous influence over economists and others in the social sciences. Utilitarianism is often the theory that is invoked when none is explicitly mentioned: for example, when people talk about what governments should do or what society should pursue.

Utilitarianism's basal space is about utilities. There are different interpretations as to what these utilities entail, but at the root of it is the idea of sets of fulfilled desires, of pleasure, wellbeing, and individual satisfaction. Jeremy Bentham and those that followed him were fundamentally concerned with how to aggregate utility across society. Their central concern was "Who gets what?" Their answer was to simply add up utility among everybody and that is what society should maximize. A fair society should be one that provides the most utility regardless of its distribution. People accordingly often refer to utilitarianism as being supremely unconcerned with inequality or distribution.

Yet, for a theory that is supremely unconcerned with inequality, utilitarianism in its most common form actually generates an optimal solution that is equal in terms of income. This means—provided people have identical utility functions that are concave—that utility diminishes as income increases. You are happier with your first increase of 10,000 euros than with the next increase. And if incomes are exogenous, that is if income is a pie to be distributed, then the optimal solution for society would be to give everybody equal shares of that pie. Even though utilitarianism itself does not care about the distribution of utility, the sum of utilities is only maximized when everybody gets the same.

However, we must produce what we distribute, whether that is income, goods, or services. Therefore, when we distribute and redistribute by taxing some and subsidizing others, the crucial question is whether we generate incentives and disincentives that might lead to a smaller pie. That would be a problem.[4]

Although utilitarianism is influential, many argue that it does not provide the answer to how we should govern our societies. One influential opponent is the libertarian writer Robert Nozick. In his *Anarchy, State, and Utopia*, Nozick argues that the fundamental problem with utilitarianism is that its focus is on distributional "end-states."[5] According to Nozick, it is not end-states that make societies fair but fair rules for the processes. Nozick's basal space is therefore much more complicated and hierarchical than simply utilities. First and foremost, he wants rights to be respected. He insists that there should be fairness in exchange and in the acquisition of wealth, assets, or income. If there have been past injustices, these should be rectified.

Among the rights he considers are the rights to owning and to bequeathing property. Accordingly, his theory tends to be considered on the right wing of the spectrum. For libertarianism, the rights to bequeath and own property are sacrosanct. Only after these rights are respected and satisfied may there be a role for the state and public policy to be concerned with utilities and other outcomes. The respect of these rights with no trade-offs is a fundamental aspect of Nozick's libertarian theory.

A different approach is provided by Rawlsian liberalism. John Rawls, whose book *A Theory of Justice* is arguably one of the most important books of all time in philosophy and the social sciences, asked the question: what social contract would societies arrive at if individuals were behind a veil of ignorance?[6] Suppose members of society are allocated different positions: landowners, industrialists, workers, or agriculturalists. What distributions would we agree on before we knew which role we would play? This idea goes back to John Harsanyi's "veil of ignorance." In John Rawls' book, the basal space are primary goods. He argues that a society that would try to arrive at a fair social contract, abstracting from people's own interests by thinking about what kind of arrangement they might want before they know their place in that arrangement, would satisfy two principles: the liberty and the opportunity principles. The liberty principle states that everyone should have as much freedom as possible, provided their freedom does not interfere with that of others. The opportunity principle then demands equal opportunities for all in the acquisition of primary goods. This is Rawls' so-called "focal combination." Subsumed within the opportunity principle is the difference principle: inequalities are permissible only if they bring the greatest benefit to those who are the worst off. This is not the same as equality if the size of the piece of the pie is different. One might ask for everybody to have the same, but then everybody ends up poor, whereas if we have less equality, the person who has the least may actually have more, in absolute terms, than in a scenario of absolute equality.

The Indian economist and philosopher Amartya Sen proposed a slightly different theory, called the Capability Approach. According to Sen, the basal space does not consist of utilities, rights, or freedoms.[7] Instead, what should be maximized is people's ability to flourish. He draws on Aristotle's notion of happiness, *euraimonia*, which may be described as the idea of a fulfilled life. Following Sen, each person gets their fulfilment by what they are able to do, by the person they are able to be. These are your functionings, and you choose these functionings from a set of possible functionings that you have, which are your capabilities. Imagine two people watching a football match over a fence. Each of them has a box to stand on, but the shorter person is still not able to watch over the fence. The shorter person's set of functionings is thus curtailed. The two people's capabilities are different. According to Sen, we should interfere by giving the shorter person a larger box to stand on. Similarly, goods and services shape capabilities and should be distributed accordingly to maximize people's ability to flourish.

Finally, I want to introduce the economic theory of equality of opportunity, which is closely related to Sen. One problem with Sen's approach is that empirically it has proven difficult to measure capability sets because they are the potential things people might be and do, and they can therefore not be observed. The equality of opportunity approach, like Sen's theory, sees a choice set more as the thing to be maximized rather than a specific point within that choice set. This choice set are opportunities. When we ask, "What is the optimal level of inequality?", the first question we must answer is, "Inequality of what?" If it is inequality of rights before the law, then there should be zero. But what about inequality of income? Do we want to live in a society where everybody is forced to have exactly the same income? What would that entail in terms of freedoms, rights, and productivity?

The theory of equality of opportunity allows for legitimate differences in outcomes that are due to choice. It does so by drawing on all the theories already discussed. It draws on libertarianism in the sense that it does take a concern with process into account. The end state is not all that matters. Obviously, it draws a lot on Rawls as well. And although equality of opportunity is described as a non-welfarist theory, it does draw to some extent on utilitarianism because it often uses individual measures of advantage, like income, as a key part of the focal combination.

The theory of equality of opportunity therefore relies on two basic principles: if you are looking to move from a given allocation to one where there is equality of opportunity, you should not compensate people for any differences in their outcomes, for example their income. People should be compensated for income differences only if these are due to factors they had no control over. Differences due to race, ethnicity, gender, place of birth, or family background, including potentially genetic differences, are factors one should be compensated for. Once we have compensated for these aspects, any remaining differences must be the individual's responsibility, for example their effort, and are legitimate. That is the principle of reward. If for example German society is divided into different groups of people that share equivalent types of circumstances, then the distribution within those groups should be equal across these types. There still can be a difference within a type because of varying effort among people. But there should not be any inequality between the types.

Today, the concept of equality of opportunity is sometimes challenged by those who demand full equality of outcomes. But we must note that equality of opportunities is actually a very radical, demanding theory. In Germany, achieving the same distribution of income across certain privileged groups as well as immigrants born from uneducated parents would require a radical transformation. What are some examples of inequality of opportunity in practice?

A first interesting example is provided by the neuroscientist Bruce Perry who compared the brain scans of two children aged three experiencing a different childhood environment, favorable and unfavorable, as defined for instance in the case of children with drug-user parents.[8] The brain scans provide evidence of the negative impact of experiencing severe neglect at home on the developing brain, which results in definitively smaller brains with more blurry structures compared to the brain scan of peers living in favorable environments. It is hard to argue that any of the developmental gaps in language, tact, and social interactions that the victim of parental neglect manifests at the age of three are due to the children's own actions. Nonetheless, in the context of contemporary American society, these two children will end up in very different places. That is inequality of opportunity.

A second illustrative example comes from a study conducted in Ecuador by Christina Paxson and Norbert Schady.[9] They analyze the determinants of pre-school-age children's scores on the Peabody Picture Vocabulary Test (PPVT), a test of language ability which measures the vocabulary of children aged three to six. The study looked at children in the wealthiest and poorest quartiles of the sample's wealth distribution, as well as children whose mothers had 12 or more years of education and those whose mothers had zero to five years of education.[10] It is shown that in Ecuador, the children of the country's wealthiest quartile and those of educated mothers stay around that expected international norm: they know the number of words one would expect them to. Children from the poorest, uneducated families, on the other hand, diverge dramatically: they have significantly lower scores than richer and more educated families' children and the gap increases with age, suggesting the presence of cumulative effects on cognitive ability. Although one may think the way to promote equal opportunities is through education, these findings show that the challenge is that there are massive gaps even before children start school.

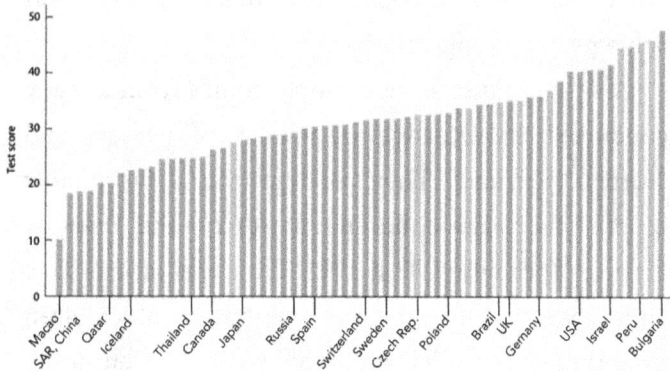

Figure 1: *Influence of parental background on secondary students' PISA test scores across countries and economies, 2009*[11]

What happens when children do start school? Figure 1, drawn from some of my work with coauthors, is based on PISA data on school achievement from the OECD Program of International Student Assessment.[12] It presents estimates of the influence of parental background on children's test scores in all the countries included in the PISA survey sample. Parental background is measured through an index of economic, social, and cultural status (ESCS), derived from questions contained in the survey about the education and occupation of one's parents, number of books present at home, etc. The association of the ESCS index with children's test scores is statistically significant.

In some cases, the impact is very large: for example, in Argentina, Bulgaria, and Peru, an improvement of one standard deviation of the index is associated with an increase of around 45 points in the test scores. Germany, too, does not fare very well, being located towards the right-hand end. Germany has an unequal distribution of wealth, and parents have a lot of influence on their children's educational path due to Germany's early tracking system in schools.

Schools are also important because of sorting: those who go to the better schools end up having better teachers and better peers. This is particularly the case in developing countries where children from rich backgrounds attend private schools.

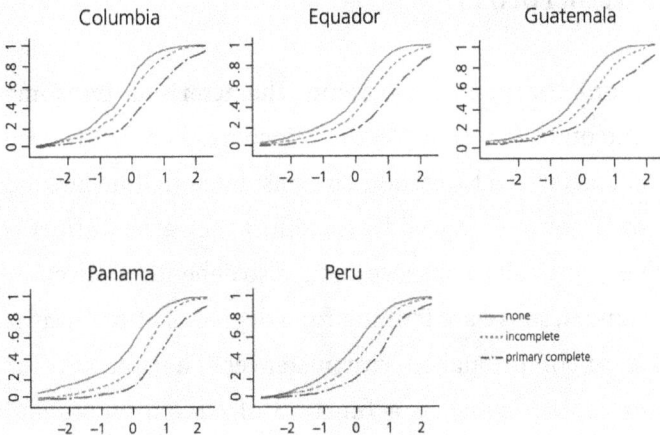

Figure 2: *The distribution of consumption conditional on mother's education*[13]

Income, of course, makes a difference as well. Figure 2 shows cumulative distribution functions in five Latin American countries.[14] The three different lines for each country represent people's household per capita consumption expenditure separated into three groups based on the education of the mother. The groups are very unequal: people whose mothers completed at least primary school are doing much better than people whose mother had an incomplete education or no education at all. These are prima facie examples of inequality of opportunity.

HOW DO ECONOMISTS MODEL INEQUALITY OF OPPORTUNITY?

Think of people as being characterized by some outcome, for example their income. People are also characterized by certain circumstances that lie beyond their control, as well by the effort they exert. Effort is very difficult to observe and it also depends on circumstances, so we are looking for a degree of effort *relative* to, or conditional on, circumstances. The outcome, for example income, is a function of circumstances and effort. Accordingly, society can be partitioned in two ways, as shown in Table 1.[15]

Types are groups of people that share the same circumstances, for example white, native German men with highly educated mothers and fathers who worked as managers. Tranches are people who exert similar degrees of effort defined in terms of being in similar percentiles of their type-specific distribution. Based on this theory we can measure inequality of opportunity.

A tranche

	e_1	e_2	e_3		e_m
C_1	x_{11}	x_{12}	x_{13}		x_{1m}
C_2	x_{21}	x_{22}	x_{23}		x_{2m}
C_3	x_{31}	x_{32}	x_{33}		x_{3m}
C_n	x_{n1}	x_{n2}	x_{n3}		x_{nm}

A type

Table 1
Source 1: Ferreira and Peragine (2016)

How do descriptions of society, built upon matrices like that in Table 1, differ from straight utilitarianism? Straight utilitarianism would have a vector order from the lowest to the highest income. It would not matter what circumstances one had. Having a matrix corrects that. Imagine a society that has only three types and plot those types as curves (Figure 3). These curves are called quantile functions and are the inverse of cumulative distribution functions. They show percentiles of the distribution within the three different types.

What is the normative theory of social justice and equality of opportunity? There are two basic approaches to this. Dirk Van de Gaer, an economist based at the University of Ghent, has argued that what society should focus on is the poorest type. We should take the value of their opportunity set, meaning the income distribution they get, and arrange society in a way that maximizes that. That means "pushing up" the poorest type ($\mu 1$): the poorest type should do as well as possible ("min-of-means" approach). American economist John Roemer says something similar, yet slightly different: the types may cross over, but we should aim to maximize income at every tranche. This is called the "mean-of-mins" approach.

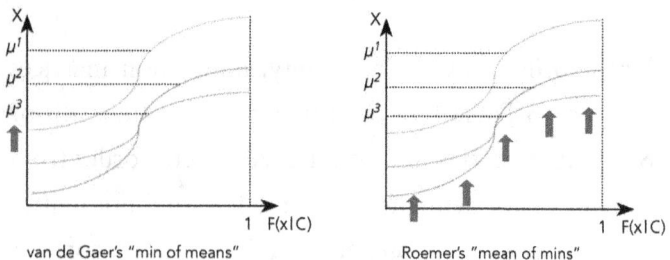

van de Gaer's "min of means"   Roemer's "mean of mins"

Figure 3

In light of these considerations, let me now try to answer the question of what the optimal level of inequality is. In work with François Bourguignon and Michael Walton, I tried to adapt the static figures in Figure 3 to a more dynamic context, capable of incorporating, for example, the concept of economic growth.[16] We argue that societies should choose a very large set of policies and regulations—including taxation and redistribution policies—so as to maximize the present discounted value of the mean of the lowest type over time, subject to the constraint of nobody being below some poverty line Z. The policy objective for opportunity egalitarians should be to maximize the future stream of income or advantage for the most disadvantaged type, while being subject to no-deprivation and policy-acceptability constraints. Figure 4 shows an annotated version of our basic objective function, noting what different parts of the formulation contribute.

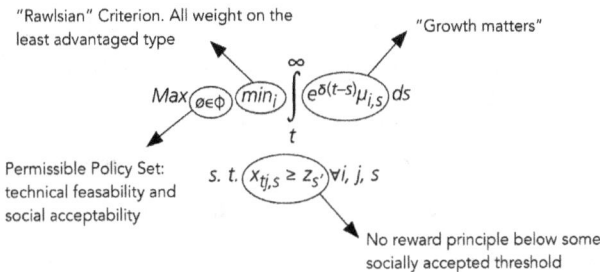

"Rawlsian" Criterion. All weight on the least advantaged type

"Growth matters"

$$Max_{\emptyset \in \phi}\ min_i \int_{t}^{\infty} \left(e^{\delta(t-s)}\mu_{i,s}\right) ds$$

Permissible Policy Set: technical feasability and social acceptability

$$s.\ t.\ \left(x_{tj,s} \geq z_{s'}\right) \forall i, j, s$$

No reward principle below some socially accepted threshold

Figure 4: *The equitable development policy problem*[17]

The formula accounts for the idea that growth matters. Future periods are aggregated over time, and the aim is to make a difference in the future. Therefore, not only the mean is taken into consideration but how those values change over time. Who are we maximizing for? The lowest type. This is the Rawlsian criterion expressed in the difference principle. And this is what makes this theory quite radical. I disagree with those who say that equality of opportunity is not a radical concept. Consider immigrants to Germany, or poor Afro-Brazilians born in slums through no fault of their own, with uneducated parents and no wealth. What we are asking for here is for society to organize itself in such a way as to maximize the future expected stream of advantages for these very underprivileged groups. This is a radical demand.

The formula includes two more aspects worth noting: first, a permissible policy set. What we mean is that feasible policies must be affordable—there is a budget constraint—but also that they must be socially acceptable. This requirement draws to some extent on Nozick and certainly a lot on Rawls' freedom and liberty principle. Policies that would violate basic rights and freedoms may not be included in the policy set. For example, we could immediately increase equality of opportunity in society by forcing the richest people to marry the poorest people, because humans tend to marry very much in assortative ways. But we do not want to tell people who to marry. Therefore, that policy is not in that set.

CONCLUSION

Deciding what the optimal level of inequality is for a society is not a simple matter. It is certainly not as simple as picking a particular value for the Gini coefficient, say 0.23 or some other such number. The optimal level of inequality arises from a broader normative consideration of how we would like society to organize itself, a consideration, in other words, of society's ultimate normative objectives. In my own view, those objectives are to give the poorest and most disadvantaged groups in society the best possible chances in the future. The optimal level of inequality is that which follows from the application of the set of policies, rules, and regulations that achieves that dynamic aim.

In practice, however, it turns out that inequality of opportunities is closely related to inequality of outcomes—both conceptually and empirically. Figure 5 below is a version of Miles Corak's Great

Gatsby Curve, and it plots a measure of inequality of opportunity against income inequality (i.e., inequality in a particular outcome).[18] The original Great Gatsby Curve uses intergenerational persistence (the opposite of mobility) instead of inequality of opportunity but, as I argue elsewhere, those two concepts are very close. Parental income is something you inherit; it is a circumstance. The difference is that our inequality of opportunity incorporates other circumstances, too. It includes race, place of birth, parental occupation, and so on. And income in the children's generation is associated with all those variables. Therefore, the notion of mobility and the notion of equality of opportunity are actually very similar.

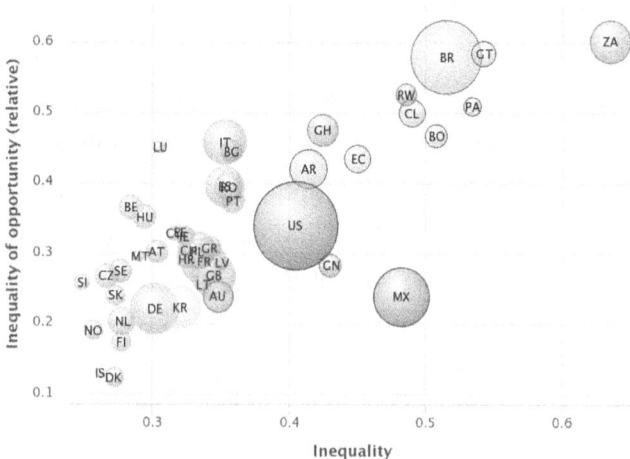

Figure 5: *Inequality of opportunity and inequality*[19]

Now, what the Great Gatsby Curve shows, whether in the mobility version or in this equality of opportunity version, is that there is a strong correlation between outcome inequality and inequality of opportunity. They are correlated because today's differences in outcomes shape tomorrow's opportunities. Whether one grows up the child of billionaires or, conversely, in a family in Baltimore's inner city, is going to shape one's opportunities in the future. Vice versa, a child's opportunities today will shape her outcomes in the future. Therefore, it is not surprising that they are deeply intertwined. Inequality of outcomes and inequality of opportunity are two sides of the same coin. But by looking only at this line, we cannot answer the question of what you should aim for, of what the optimal level is. I argue that to answer the question of the optimal level, we must try to solve the complex normative problem discussed earlier.

Notes

1. This paper is a lightly edited transcript of a lecture delivered at a Convoco! Forum in Berlin on April 26, 2022. While I am very grateful to Annaelena Valentini for invaluable assistance in editing the transcript, I take full responsibility for the content.

2. World Bank Group, *Poverty an͘ Share͘ Prosperity 2016: Taking on Inequality* (Washington, DC: World Bank, 2016).

3. Ibid., p. 84.

4. This is a fundamental trade-off in economics, famously discussed by Arthur M. Okun in his book *Equality an͘ Efficiency: The Big Tra͘eoff* (Washington DC: Brookings Institution Press, 1975).

5. Robert Nozick, *Anarchy, State, an͘ Utopia* (New York: Basic Books, 1974).

6. John Rawls, *A Theory of Justice* (Cambridge, MA: Harvard University Press, 1971).

7. Amartya Sen, "Equality of what?" in *The Tanner Lectures on Human Values*, ed. Sterling McMurrin (Salt Lake City: University of Utah Press, 1980).

8. Bruce D. Perry, "Childhood experience and the expression of genetic potential: what childhood neglect tells us about nature and nurture" in *Brain an͘ Min͘* 3 (1), 2002, pp. 79–100.

9. Christina Paxson and Norbert Schady, "Cognitive Development among Young Children in Ecuador: The Roles of Wealth, Health, and Parenting" in *Journal of Human Resources* 42 (1), 2007, pp. 49–84.

10. This is not a representative sample, since it's already a sample from a poor neighbourhood.

11. Francisco H. G. Ferreira, Julian Messina, Jamele Rigolini, Luis Felipe López-Calva, Maria Ana Lugo, and Renos Vakis, *Economic Mobility an͘ the Rise of the Latin American Mi͘͘le Class* (Washington, DC: World Bank Publications, 2012).

12. Ibid.

13. Francisco H. G. Ferreira, and Jérémie Gignoux, "The Measurement of Inequality of Opportunity: Theory and an Application to Latin America" in *Review of Income and Wealth* 57 (4), 2011, pp. 622–57.

14. Ibid.

15. Francisco H. G. Ferreira, and Vito Peragine, "Individual Responsibility and Equality of Opportunity" in *The Oxford Handbook of Well-being and Public Policy*, ed. Matthew D. Adler and Marc Fleurbaey (Oxford: Oxford University Press, 2016).

16. François Bourguignon, Francisco H. G. Ferreira, and Michael Walton, "Equity, efficiency and inequality traps: A research agenda" in *Journal of Economic Inequality* 5 (2), 2007, pp. 235–56.

17. Ibid.

18. Miles Corak, "Inequality from Generation to Generation: The United States in Comparison" in *The Economics of Inequality, Poverty, and Discrimination in the 21st Century*, ed. Robert Rycroft (Santa Barbara, CA: ABC-CLIO, 2013), pp.107–26.

19. Equal chances, *The World Database on Equality of Opportunity and Social Mobility* (beta version, May 2018).

CHAPTER 2

DISTRIBUTIVE AND SOCIAL EQUALITY

JONATHAN WOLFF

Within contemporary political philosophy, there are two main ways of thinking about equality: one is what we can call "distributive" and the other "social" (or "relational") equality. Distributive equality, of which economic equality is one variant, is concerned with ensuring an equal distribution of something. Academic debate here has focused on the question: what it is that we're worried about. What is the thing that should be distributed equally? Is it money, happiness, standard of living, or something different altogether? The distributive question is about the ways in which the world is unequal in those respects. It is about who gets what, and whether that is equal.

When I started out as a political philosopher, many of my teachers and the people who had influenced me were working on this question of distributive equality, putting forward different ideas and arguments for them. But I was always a bit uneasy about that because what attracted me to the idea of equality didn't seem to be so much a question of whether everyone had the same income or the same goods. I was interested in how people relate to each other, how we regard each other in society. Are we living in a society where some people are having to look up and others are looking down? This is a notion of social equality rather than distributive equality. When I eventually came to formulate my own views, I realized what I was interested in was not so much what it means to have an *equal ɩistribution*, but what it is to have a *society of equals*, which may or may not be the same as equal distribution. What is the fundamental nature of an equal society? Is it one where things are shared out fairly? Or is it one where people relate to each other in particular ways? Or is it both and these aspects are related?

In the following I want to discuss how I came to this way of thinking and consider some of the problems that remain with this approach. I'm going to start at what may seem a strange place to start, namely the notion of equality of opportunity.

Equality of opportunity is one of the most popular ideas in contemporary political life, perhaps even everywhere in the world. Few people would say that they are not in favor of equality of opportunity. But would they all agree on what equality of opportunity means? As a term, equality of opportunity can stand for many different ideas. Let me begin by introducing three different ways of understanding equality of opportunity, before complicating matters by adding a fourth.

The first notion of equality of opportunity is a simple one of antidiscrimination. The idea is that if you advertise for a job, for example, you should consider only the applicants' qualifications and abilities. You should not pay any attention to the color of their skin, their religion, or other irrelevant attributes. We know that we are far from achieving equality of opportunity even in this minimal sense. There's been a lot of research on the scenario where people have sent in essentially the same CVs for job applications, but with different names revealing ethnic identities, or different photographs showing black or white skin, or a head scarf suggesting religious affiliation and so on. And, as far as I know, in every place these studies have been done, the person who looks most like a member of the majority ethnicity or culture is much more likely to be called for an interview than another who is not, even if the CVs are identical. Discrimination still exists today, although I think—I hope—it is probably mostly implicit rather than explicit. People perhaps are picking up cues that they're not even aware of. Nevertheless, even on this first level of equality of opportunity, antidiscrimination, we've still got a long way to go.

The second understanding of equality of opportunity takes the thought of antidiscrimination further. Suppose people have different opportunities to acquire a good CV. Some people don't have the same educational opportunities, as they may have attended schools that were poorly resourced in comparison to others. Is that fair? This example is a constant subject of debate at my university, Oxford University. Should we compensate in our admissions for people who've had a poorer educational background, or is that unfair to others? Should there be a lottery? Should we provide some sort of remedial education because we're trying to make the competition fairer by allowing people to acquire the same qualifications? This is the second level of equality of opportunity. Whereas the first level was simply antidiscrimination, this second level additionally requires equality of education.

Yet we can still go further—to a third idea of equality of opportunity—because even if people have the same educational opportunities, life is not constituted only by being at school. What happens in one's home life can be even more important than what happens at school. Naturally we think here of people with the advantages of wealth and those who may have grown up in poverty as a comparison. But interesting research suggests that other aspects of our home life can also be unexpectedly fateful. For example, there is a very strong correlation between being read bedtime stories as a child and doing well in later life. There are many complicated layers of causation as to why that may be. But we can see that things outside our control can affect equality of opportunities. And this is something that is going to be very hard for governments to correct.

The most radical notions of equality of opportunity, then, argue that in addition to antidiscrimination and equality of education, we must take home life and family background somehow into account and neutralize their influence on opportunity. Only then we will have achieved a world in which, to put it in the words of the American philosopher John Rawls, people with the same talent and the same motivation have the same chances of achieving successful positions. This way of thinking about equality of opportunity is much more radical than anything we have achieved in society. And I think it's probably more radical than what we can achieve even if we put all our effort into it. As Rawls himself says, for as long as the family exists, we will never achieve full equality of opportunity because people will grow up in different family circumstances.

The reason I chose to take these detours through equality of opportunity is that following this path we end up in a position that converges with a particular theory of distributive equality. This theory—sometimes now called "luck egalitarianism"—states that people should be completely equal unless their own free choices lead to inequality. We should compensate people if they have bad luck in life, but if they make bad choices, that's their own responsibility. Therefore, we should equalize background circumstances as much as we can, and then let people make their own decisions to bring about success in life or not. Here we have a notion of distributive equality that demands for everything to be shared equally unless there are good reasons for inequality. And those good reasons can only be people's individual effort and talent. The theory combines a view of individual responsibility with a background theory of equality of opportunity. For a long time, this was the dominant theory in thinking about equality in left-wing political philosophy, the theory that I was most acquainted with as a graduate student and as a junior academic. But as mentioned above, I wasn't convinced by this theory. What were my reservations?

One might argue that this theory is simply impossible to bring about in practice. This is an important objection, of course, but as philosophers we can think about ideas even if we can't fully bring them into reality. Two other problems are for me central. For the first problem, we must return to the third definition of equality of opportunity, which states that people of similar talents and motivation should have the same chances for the opportunities and resources of society. In other words, people should be placed on a level playing field. This is a very common expression. But when do we need a level playing field? We need one if we are in a race, in a competition. Equality of opportunity understood this way thus presupposes that life is a race for scarce goods. What we're trying to do is make life as fair as possible for people to compete for those prized positions or rare goods in society. To see what's wrong with that, consider the opportunities of children.

I assume that many parents today want to give their children a life of rich opportunity. But what do we mean by that? Do we want them to be first in every race they run, come top of the class, or be the best piano player? Maybe some do, but for many of us what we really want is for our children to be able to sample many opportunities and find out what suits them. Your children may want to go to a drama class, experience different sports, try out playwriting, or learn to sing. But crucially these are all things that every child could do because they are not competitive. Therefore, I want to introduce a distinction between competitive opportunity and non-competitive opportunity. Take swimming as another example. Children may want to swim to compete in races where only one child wins a prize. But there is also something else you could do in swimming. When I was a child in the UK there was something called the "green badge." At the time this was a national scheme whereby you had to jump into the water in your pajamas, take them off, tread water for 30 seconds, and then swim a length. Then, like me, you got the green badge. If you did something more demanding, you got the yellow badge, then the blue badge, and so on. But the fact that one child was awarded a green badge didn't mean there were fewer green badges to go around. Every child could have a green badge. This is another sense of opportunity that I feel is more enriching. It's not about making the conditions fair for a race, but rather giving everyone the opportunity to flourish in their own way or to achieve things which are not necessarily competitive.

It's very peculiar to me that people who are interested in equality would want to reduce equality to a fair competition in a race for scarce positions. Wouldn't it be much better to try to envisage a world in which we get away from competition and think about it in a more "hippie fashion" where everyone should have prizes? And these prizes are not worthless. The swimming badge is not given away for nothing. You have to work for it. And with that certificate your life might be a bit better, maybe because you can go on a certain type of holiday you wouldn't have been allowed to before. An adult version of the green badge is the drivers' license. There is no limit to how many are issued, and with it you can do valuable things that you wouldn't be able to do without it. In sum, we can give people the opportunity to acquire things that will help in life and that don't rule out other people doing the same.

That was my objection to conceiving of equality in terms of making background conditions fair: it makes life seem too much like a competition. Now to my second reservation about this idea of equality of opportunity: the key notion of theory of equality as I've described it is that if your situation is down to your choices or your effort, you get the benefits or disadvantages. If it's a matter of bad luck on the other hand, you get some sort of compensation from the state. This may seem very fair and reasonable. But I want to convince you that fairness can come at too high a price. Take unemployment benefit, for example. Societies that follow this type of approach to equality of opportunity will say, "Yes, you can have unemployment benefit, but only if you are unemployed through no fault of your own." The consequence is that there has to be a test to see if the person in question could work. We need some way of working out who is at fault for their situation and who is not at fault.

This thought is very close to means testing or capacity testing. My mother was a receptionist for a doctor when, unfortunately, she caught tuberculosis from one of the patients. She was entitled to disability benefits for several years as a result. But every year she had to prove that she was disabled. Doctors would come from the city to our small village and those claiming disability benefit would have to line up outside the village hall to take turns to demonstrate that they were unable to work. In my mother's case, because she had suffered from a lung disease, she had to take off all her clothes and blow into a bag to show her chest expansion in front of three male doctors that she had never met before to prove she was disabled.

The experience was utterly humiliating for her. What sort of society puts people through this? It's not a society that believes in my idea of equality. It's a society that wants to make sure people don't cheat the system. Society uses a lot of its resources setting up gateposts to stop people taking advantage of the rest. It's incredible how much we spend trying to catch free riders when instead we could say, "Yes, some people might exploit us, but we can put up with that. It's a more humane society in which we allow some free riding instead of investing 2–5 percent of GDP into trying to stop people cheating."

These are of course experimental questions; perhaps exploitation of the system would increase much more if we were to follow this path. But these two problems, that equality of opportunity is competitive in the way I described it and that it requires us to have humiliating capacity testing for the people we're trying to help, have pushed me into a different way of thinking about equality. I argue that equality is really about respect for everyone rather than the distribution of things. We need to think about what it means to live in a society of equals. What are these relations of equality that happen between individuals? Is it just being courteous and polite to each other, or is there something more we can say about positive relations of equality? This is a very difficult question, and there is no settled consensus on the nature of the relations that constitute a society of equals. And what I shall say about it may seem rather disappointing, perhaps even a cheat.

One thing that is very clear for people like me who believe in social equality is that we know what we're against. We know what social *inequality* looks like. Social inequality includes discrimination, exploitation, hierarchy, dominance, social exclusion, oppression, and violence. There are many ways in which societies can be socially unequal. My approach is to say that this realization is all we need. With a theory of social inequality, we've got plenty of work to do to eliminate instances of social inequality without having to worry too much about what a perfect society of social equality would be. That is to say, we can pay attention to gross social inequalities without having a determinate answer to the question of what a society of social equality would be.

This may seem surprising, or perhaps even impossible. It is a common suspicion that we cannot talk about the negative unless we've got a theory of the positive. How can we talk about inequality unless we've got a theory of equality? This is a fascinating issue, and I'll give you the short answer: we can and do, even when we don't have a full theory. Consider the example of exploitation which I suggested is one form of social inequality. Almost all of us have seen conditions of work we regard as unjust because they're exploitative. But do any of us have a theory of exploitation that explains why certain things are exploitative or not, or, to put it another way, have a view about the cutoff between exploitative and nonexploitative working conditions? I suspect hardly anyone who uses the term has such a theory. We seem perfectly capable of pointing out exploitation without having a theory of where exploitation ends. There may be grey areas, but people think they can identify clear instances of injustice without having a theory of justice. It's not dissimilar to having a sense of grammar for your own language. Someone once asked me when to use "some" and when to use "any" in English. I had no idea there was the possibility of confusion or a rule for using these words in English—it had never occurred to me. But despite having no idea what the rule is, I got it right all the time. And if I saw examples of people using the words incorrectly, I would have been able to pick up on it. We can have an instinct for when things go wrong without having a theory about what would be right. I argue that in that same way we can think about equality and justice by focusing on the negative. And we can do that either because we don't think there is a positive or, in a more concessionary way, we believe that we can make a lot of progress by focusing on the way the world goes wrong rather than thinking about what a perfect world would be.

Two final comments: I have said that people who believe in social equality are opposed to the idea of hierarchy. Often, I get questioned on this point: How can we have a society without hierarchy? For example, could there be an army or a business without hierarchy? I can agree that there are good reasons for having individual hierarchies in our society. What I oppose, however, are group hierarchies such as class or caste. These are types of group relations where one group regards themselves as superior to another group. And I have never heard a good argument for why there should be group hierarchies in society. The only argument that I know of is that we cannot get rid of it. That may be true, but that doesn't mean that we shouldn't take as many steps as we can to mitigate the problem.

Finally, there was an intriguing question connected to Convoco's topic for 2022, namely "What is the optimum level of inequality?" This is not a question that's easy for me to answer because I don't think of equality and inequality in quantitative terms. There isn't a number to put on how socially unequal society is—or should be. I think of equality and inequality as multi-faceted. Society can be equal in some respects, for example, no hierarchy, but unequal in others, for example, social exclusion of individuals or exploitation. And in this view the idea of an optimum level of inequality is a strange question. With some exceptions around the necessity of hierarchy for organizational purposes, inequality is generally to be opposed, even if some inequalities are more urgent than others, and some can only be mitigated but never completely eradicated.

CHAPTER 3

EQUALITY IN THE LAW

MARIETTA AUER

Equality has probably been one of the most debated legal problems since antiquity.[1] Since the advent of European legal thought, the answer to the question of who should be treated as equal to whom, in what respect, and what should be the legal consequences of unequal treatment, has been in constant flux. In order to understand the development of equality theory in the law until the present day, we must first distinguish between formal and material concepts of equality. We can then focus on the relationship between freedom and equality in liberal legal theory. Historically, we can distinguish on this basis between two stages of claims to the creation of equality in the law.[2] In the first stage, since the Enlightenment, aspirations have aimed at eliminating group-related forms of discrimination (based on characteristics such as sex, race, and religion) and at establishing formal legal equality for all people. Recently, a second stage of efforts at achieving equality is no longer concerned with reducing formal kinds of discrimination, but rather with changing social power structures with the aim of achieving real, substantive equality for previously disadvantaged groups. Against this background, the question arises whether and to what extent the creation of such material equality, beyond the elimination of formal discrimination, can be a fundamental task of the law.

I. FORMAL AND MATERIAL FREEDOM AND EQUALITY

We can talk about equality in both a formal and a material sense. What this distinction means becomes clear if we first consider the parallel distinction between formal and material freedom. A *formal* concept of freedom requires the guarantee of purely legal freedom granted equally to everyone regardless of status. A *material* concept of freedom, on the other hand, takes into account the actual chances of realizing the freedom in question. Freedom, in this sense, is interpreted as the actual freedom of choice, including all the legal consequences attached to that choice. For instance, in cases of seriously unequal bargaining power, there would be a demand for an equalization via the creation of contractual parity.

Just as in the sphere of legal freedom, a similar distinction can be made between a formal concept of equality, meaning formal legal equality, and a material notion of the concept, meaning actual equality. In other words, we can talk about both a *first* and a *secon* problem of freedom and equality.[3] The first problem of freedom and equality marks the beginning of the egalitarian understanding of law in modernity, which is primarily concerned with the abolition of feudal status law and the creation of a general legal capacity applying to all persons qua personhood. The second problem of freedom and equality, on the other hand, only comes to light when this first stage has been mastered and it becomes apparent that formal equal freedom in no way results in like chances of realizing individual claims to freedom and equality. To effect change and bring about real freedom and real equality, a considerable amount of effort is still necessary.

Yet the latter already bears an insight that needs to be considered in the following analysis: Freedom and equality are not in and of themselves desirable; instead, their value is derived from their respective inherent degree of justice. In the end, all considerations of formal or material freedom—or equality—aim at a specific conception of justice. Such concepts can also be interpreted either formally or materially. While formal—one could even say procedural—concepts of justice focus on equality of opportunity, material aspirations to justice pursue equality of outcome. Procedural notions of justice play a central role not only in the philosophical works of thinkers such as John Rawls and Jürgen Habermas, but they also feature prominently in modern democratic decision-making processes. The realization of claims to justice in pluralistic societies requires more than simply specifying substantive goals in terms of equality. Procedural justice can accomplish this by guaranteeing both equality of initial opportunities and the fairness of the legal process. In liberal societies, a material concept of freedom—not a material concept of justice—is required to reach procedurally *justifie* decisions. Equality of opportunity is both necessary and sufficient to serve as a benchmark of justice. Equality of outcome, by contrast, is neither achievable nor legitimate as a broad objective of law in liberal societies.

Following from this, we glean the first important insight of this analysis: Freedom and equality, as prerequisites of justice in modern societies, do not exhibit a common structure. Freedom, in accordance with its structure, can serve as a self-legitimizing principle of justice precisely when it is conceived in formal terms and devoid of any content. And herein lies the core of all conceptions of justice that prioritize freedom over equality.

Equality, on the other hand, exhibits a very different structure. Unlike freedom, it always requires a qualitative, material fulfilment in accordance with a given standard of equal treatment. When it comes to gender, for instance, questions such as the following suggest themselves: Are we talking about equal legal capacity for men and women? Equal voting rights? Equal representation on electoral lists, boards, or supervisory board positions? Same-sex marriage? Equality in adoption rights? Non-binary gender rights? Transgender rights? This characteristically results in a situation where possible claims to equal treatment— bar those aiming at a complete and in reality unachievable equality, which paradoxically are not (and cannot be) the point of the law—are limitless and ultimately can never be attained. It is no secret that this represents the Achilles heel of modern equal treatment and anti-discrimination law, especially in societies in which egalitarian principles have already been widely put into practice.

II. EQUALITY AND FREEDOM IN ENLIGHTENMENT PHILOSOPHY

The foregoing analysis has made clear that equality in the law cannot be thought of as an absolute. Instead, in liberal societies, it must always be coordinated with the at least partially conflicting principle of freedom. This countervailing principle of freedom does not aim at the greatest possible degree of equal treatment. To the contrary, it embraces the freely chosen opportunity of (self-)differentiation. The asymmetrical relationship exhibited by freedom and equality becomes all the more apparent when considering the foundations of the idea of universal equality in Enlightenment philosophy. Modern law, in particular private law, is essentially based on the Enlightenment concept of the social contract. This concept stipulates that the only valid way to establish legitimate state institutions possessing normatively valid law-making and law-enforcement powers is a contract concluded between all members of the society as free and equal parties. The same basic idea holds true on a smaller scale. The freely concluded contract, regardless of its content, has a self-legitimating effect not only as a social contract but also as a consensus of wills between private individuals, precisely because it was concluded between equals acting in a free and self-responsible fashion. Both on the macro level of constitutional law and on the micro level of private law, the contract principle can be described without exaggeration as the most powerful legitimizing principle of modern law.

The basis of the universal legitimizing power of the contract principle, as already found in Immanuel Kant, is the maxim *"volenti non fit iniuria."* This maxim asserts that no harm can come to a willing person, irrespective of the content of the contract, because and insofar as the person consents. The form of consent itself thus replaces the evaluation of the content of consent by means of the mechanism of freely responsible consent. This is expressed even more strongly in the maxim *"stat pro ratione voluntas,"* according to which the pure form of the will takes the place of the rationality of the intended content.[4] The basis of this principle of will is the Enlightenment idea that only human reason can be regarded the source of interpersonally valid norms—for only reason is equally available to all rational beings. Therefore, equality in the sense of Enlightenment rationalism isn't just any kind of equality. It is to be understood as a specific equality in the ability to use reason and freedom, i.e., what belongs equally to all rational human beings. That human beings differ in their individual characteristics and capacities—even when it comes to group characteristics often prone to discrimination such as gender, descent, etc.—is simply of no consequence from the perspective of Enlightenment legal thinking. Much like the empirical differences in individual abilities to make use of freedom, these differentiating characteristics are *by definition* irrelevant, because all that matters for participation in the rational mechanism of legitimation is the equality of all people—as equals in their personhood—under the law. Even if three hundred years ago it would never have occurred to the architects of these ideas to grant women or slaves the same civil legal capacity as white men of European descent, "all people" now really means *all* people. The revolutionary power of the Enlightenment mechanism of legitimation lies precisely in the fact that it has developed its own unstoppable historical-normative momentum ever since its initial formulation, a directional dynamic toward the ever-increasing realization of the claim to universalization inscribed within it.

On this basis, it is certainly correct to speak of a "preponderance of freedom over equality" in a strictly qualified sense. Even though it is true that the Enlightenment mechanism of legitimation always presupposes equality in the sense of an equal innate capacity for reason, contracts are valid not simply because they have been agreed upon between equals, but only *if* and *when* these contracts have genuinely been concluded in a free, self-determined manner by these equals. In that case, the legitimizing mechanism *always* lies in freedom and not in equality. No allocative or distributive decision can be considered legitimate merely because everyone is treated equally. Decisive here is the normative Enlightenment claim to submit all heteronomous systems of justice—whether they are based on God, nature, or the social order, with its contingent power structures—to a critique of reason and replace them with the only indisputable principle of legitimacy of modern society: the principle of individual autonomy. Although Enlightenment thinking always presupposes equality, the true driver of all its conceptions of justice remains freedom.

III. FORMAL LEGAL EQUALITY: THE FIRST
EQUALITY PROBLEM

What implications does this have for equality as a legal goal? Without a doubt, there is a considerable difference between the theoretical preconditions of the Enlightenment concepts of freedom and equality described above and their actual historical implementation in law since the turn to modernity. The modern legal struggle for equality began with centuries of disputes about the recognition of universal formal equality. These struggles—referred to above as the first equality problem—are still ongoing in many parts of the world. Regarding this struggle, the milestones of the past 200 years of legal history involve, on the one hand, the extension of formal equal treatment to women, which, for example, was not realized in German family law until well into the second half of the 20th century. On the other hand, they encompass the arduous dismantling of disenfranchisement resulting from discrimination according to the persisting and recurring patterns of sex and gender, race and ethnicity, religion and belief. In this context, the formal disenfranchisement of entire population groups through sovereign decisions that deliberately and systematically withheld basic rights, such as life, health, physical integrity, freedom of expression, and freedom of movement, from discriminated sections of the population had a particularly dramatic impact. The same applies to the discriminatory inaccessibility of private and public status rights as granted by citizenship, immigration, civil status, or family law. Under modern law, the method of choice for dismantling such patterns of formal discrimination have been constitutional principles of equality, such as those laid down in the Virginia Declaration of Rights of 1776 or France's *Déclaration ‹es Droits ‹e l'Homme et ‹u Citoyen* of 1789. Modern guarantees of equality such as Art. 3 of Germany's Basic Law often supplement the general equal treatment clause with specific prohibitions on discrimination that explicitly state the impermissibility of certain differentiation criteria such as sex, race, language, county of origin, religion, or disability.

An important lesson to be drawn from the historical experience of extremely unjust regimes, such as the fascist and Stalinist dictatorships of Europe, colonial slave-owning societies, and modern apartheid regimes, is that the general principle of equality—as laid down in modern constitutions that have enshrined universal formal equality and legitimizing freedom—actually captures the core of what one can and should meaningfully understand by justice under the rule of law. This reading is confirmed by the second subsection of the so-called Radbruch Formula, formulated by Gustav Radbruch, a legal philosopher and Minister of Justice in the Weimar Republic. The relevant subsection of this formula reads: "Where justice is not even strived for, where equality, which is the core of justice, is renounced in the process of legislation, there a statute is not just 'erroneous law,' it is in fact not of a legal nature at all. That is because law, even positive law, cannot be defined otherwise than as a rule, that is precisely intended to serve justice."[5] Radbruch is absolutely right: justice essentially means equality.

IV. FROM LEGAL EQUALITY TO EQUALITY OF STATUS: THE SECOND EQUALITY PROBLEM

All of this leads us back to the question raised earlier: equality of what?[6] More precisely, in what respect and in what ways is the legal system responsible not only for formal equality but should work towards the actual equality of all those subject to the law as well? This question brings into focus the second equality problem described above. Only recently has this problem been addressed as a specific issue of legal regulation for promoting substantive equality, thus highlighting the historical variability of legal aspirations to equal treatment. In European Union law, the turning point came in the first decade of the new millennium. Since 2000, European legislators have issued several directives on equal treatment, which have served as the engine of European non-discrimination law ever since. While their impact is particularly apparent in labor law, the scope of these directives reaches far beyond into the sphere of general private law. Germany's General Equal Treatment Act (*Allgemeines Gleichbehan*‌*lungsgesetz*) of 2007 was one of the national laws enacted on the basis of these directives. When the Act came into force, reactions in the legal literature varied considerably. Some responded with harsh critique, while other welcomed it as a paradigm shift towards the recognition of a general principle of equal treatment under private law. A simultaneous dynamic developed in family law after the introduction of the civil partnership law, which in Germany in 2017 led to the introduction of same-sex marriage (*Ehe für alle*). The implementation of gender equality goals in the business world also enjoys a high priority in German politics. In order to promote women to management positions, Germany has enacted two Management Position Acts (*Führungspositionengesetze*) since 2015, which, among other things, provide for binding gender quotas for appointments to supervisory and executive boards of publicly listed and co-determined companies. Despite such efforts, however, actual progress towards gender equality has been modest. According to the World Economic Forum's Global Gender Gap Report of 2021, if progress continues at the current rate, it will take around 135 years for the global gender gap to close.[7]

Yet, all of these regulations—apart from the disputed question of their practical efficacy—still do not answer the question at hand: To what extent should the realization of actual equality be a legal goal at all? Total equality, even when viewed from the refined normative aspirations of the new millennium, cannot be the goal of a liberally constituted society. This already follows from the fact that classic constitutional liberties such as freedom of ownership and freedom of occupation protect precisely the freedom of *individuals to develop differently*. The principle of freedom, even when it translates into economic and social inequality by means of private law, cannot be dismissed as mere bourgeois ideology.[8] Freedom is granted to the benefit of everyone, because individual differences—such as the development of different talents, the realization of different lifestyles, as well as any form of competitive development of individual and social goals—are socially desirable in a pluralistic society. We commit a logical fallacy if we, on the one hand, enjoy the advantages of individualization, pluralization, and economic freedom of activity, but, on the other, don't want to pay the price, i.e., the acceptance and dynamic self-reinforcement of individual and group-specific differences. It therefore conveys a distorted picture if we describe the first and second equality problem as a continuum of steadily increasing fulfilment of aspirations to justice, whose hypothetical culmination lies in the total establishment of legal and factual equality in all conceivable aspects. This ultimate goal is unattainable.

V. A UNIVERSAL RIGHT TO EQUAL TREATMENT?

In a society that is pluralistic but, nevertheless, sees itself as egalitarian, this shifts the question to ask which inequalities are normatively undesirable to such an extent that they are felt to be in need of correction *beyon* the elimination of formal discrimination. At this point, the historical variability and contingency of social aspirations to legal equality become apparent once again. The tense relationship between equality and freedom in liberal societies has no historically stable point of equilibrium. Rather, claims to equality, especially in the area of private law, continue to clash with the conceptually defining freedom to shape one's own relationships through private law. Against this background, not only does the emptiness of the general principle of equality come into focus once again, but it should also become intuitively clear, structurally speaking, why the goal of material equality, especially in contexts of private law, was not recognized as a main objective in legal policy until the first decade of the new millennium.

Has this assessment changed in light of the current status of national and European equal treatment directives and non-discrimination law? Michael Grünberger has recently advocated this thesis in German private law theory. He claims that the classical view of the primacy of freedom over equality, when seen against the backdrop of the current state of private law right to equal treatment, was no longer a convincing description of the existing state of law. In contrast, Grünberger argues that the tension between freedom and equality in private law should be resolved in favor of equality and *not* freedom.[9] When seen in the context of current debates about sexism, racism, and the colonial legacies of Western thought, Grünberger has certainly exposed a weak spot in the classical doctrine, which, in part, explicitly emphasizes the "freedom to discriminate" as the core value of private autonomy.[10] Against this, one could indeed argue that a society governed by a private law which emphatically professes the value of discrimination is neither likely to have a promising future nor worth living in.

Yet the question arises whether this normative disaffection, itself bound to the zeitgeist of the time, is sufficient to justify the purported adoption of a general principle of equal treatment under private law. Conceptually, this would mean that any unequal treatment would need to be justified, even between private individuals. If one assumes that this is true, the libertarian contract law maxim *stat pro ratione voluntas* no longer holds. At this point, however, the question arises whether the national and European anti-discrimination and equal treatment laws discussed above merit such a conceptually far-reaching conclusion. Their normative pattern, scattered over various legislative acts, sufficiently shows that the question of the normative relevance of equality problems can only be addressed in a context-dependent manner, that is, with regard to a specific feature and measured against a specific comparison group. Against this, it cannot be maintained that the normative structure of freedom is empty as well, unless its content is concretized through individual cases concerning the actual use of freedom. The main insight here is that the law not only protects context-dependent individual freedoms, but also (and in particular) the abstract, indeterminate principle of freedom as the source of future innovations of freedom.

Therein lies a crucial difference from equality. The constitutional principle of equal treatment and the specific prohibitions of anti-discrimination law do not protect any and all future innovations of equality. All equal treatment laws discussed above contain precise enumerations of the prohibited cases of discrimination. It may be true that the constitutional principle of equal treatment, nonetheless, makes it possible to identify and address new problems of equality. However, it is anything but a foregone conclusion that all new and yet to be discussed future claims for equal treatment always automatically possess a presumptive added value in terms of social justice or expedience. And it is insufficient to simply respond that the same holds for the scope of future freedoms. To return to the beginning of this analysis, freedom—in contrast to equality—carries a principle of legitimacy within it. The pathos of freedom—and only of freedom—consists in conferring upon persons who are formally equal in their ability to reason the decision about their own normative goals and freeing them from having God, nature, or the well-intentioned state decide how they are to live their lives. The empty space of freedom is a principle of legitimacy. The empty space of equality is just that—empty.

Notes

1. See Aristotle, *Nichomachean Ethics*, book V, chapter VI.

2. For more detail, see Michael Grünberger, *Personale Gleichheit* (Baden-Baden: Nomos, 2013), pp. 29 ff.; Anna Katharina Mangold, *Demokratische Inklusion ⸱urch Recht. Anti⸱iskriminierungsrecht als Ermöglichungsbe⸱ingung ⸱er ⸱emokratischen Begegnung von Freien un⸱ Gleichen* (Tübingen: Mohr Siebeck, 2021), pp. 182 ff.; on the whole subject, see also Marietta Auer, "Zwei Jahrhunderte Privatrechtstheorie zu formaler und materialer Gleichheit" in Stefan Grundmann and Jan Thiessen (eds.), *Von formaler zu materialer Gleichheit* (Tübingen: Mohr Siebeck, 2021), pp. 67 ff.

3. Grünberger, *Personale Gleichheit*, pp. 113 ff.

4. For a fundamental discussion, see Immanuel Kant, *Metaphysical First Principles of the Doctrine of Right*, § 46; from the perspective of private law, see Werner Flume, *Allgemeiner Teil ⸱es Bürgerlichen Rechts*, vol. 2: *Das Rechtsgeschäft*, 4th edn. (Berlin: Springer, 1992), pp. 1 ff.

5. Gustav Radbruch, "Gesetzliches Unrecht und übergesetzliches Recht" in *Sü⸱⸱eutsche Juristenzeitung* (1946), pp. 105, 107; translation: https://en.wikipedia.org/wiki/ Radbruch_formula (accessed December 9, 2022). Original: "Wo Gerechtigkeit nicht einmal erstrebt wird, wo die

Gleichheit, die den Kern der Gerechtigkeit ausmacht, bei der Setzung positiven Rechts bewusst verleugnet wurde, da ist das Gesetz nicht etwa nur 'unrichtiges' Recht, vielmehr entbehrt es überhaupt der Rechtsnatur. Denn man kann Recht, auch positives Recht, gar nicht anders definieren als eine Ordnung und Satzung, die ihrem Sinne nach bestimmt ist, der Gerechtigkeit zu dienen."

6. On the question "equality of what?", see also Amartya Sen, *Inequality Reexamined* (Cambridge, MA: Harvard University Press, 1995), p. 11.

7. World Economic Forum, *Global Gender Gap Report 2021*, p. 5, https://www3.weforum.org/docs/WEF_GGGR_2021.pdf (accessed December 9, 2022).

8. For an eloquent analysis, see Katharina Pistor, *The Code of Capital. How the Law Creates Wealth and Inequality* (Princeton/Oxford: Princeton University Press, 2019).

9. Grünberger, *Personale Gleichheit*, pp. 749 ff.

10. Karl Riesenhuber, "Privatautonomie – Rechtsprinzip oder mystifizierendes 'Leuchtfeuer'"? in *Zeitschrift für die gesamte Privatrechtswissenschaft* (2018), pp. 352, 366.

CHAPTER 4

EQUALITY IN AN UNEQUAL WORLD: HISTORICAL PERSPECTIVES

JÖRN LEONHARD

I. HISTORICAL ORIGINS: GROUP-DEFINED EQUALITY IN A WORLD DETERMINED BY INEQUALITY

Whether institutionalized socially, politically, legally, or religiously, inequality was the norm in the periods preceding the end of the 18th century. For example, imperial rule was based on distinct hierarchies and explicit inequality between "barbarians" and "civilized people," between "invaders" and the indigenous population. Degrees of inequality between central areas and peripheries resulted from the coexistence of ethnic, religious, and legal diversity. Inequality was also a fundamental feature of European societies based on old estates, characterized by corporatist structures and privileges based on birthright. Within these worlds defined by inequality, membership of a particular group was formed simultaneously by equality based on corporatist identity and the corresponding practices of differentiation and symbolic self-assertion. For example, the active members of the ancient *polis* generally enjoyed the political equality of active participation among themselves, while unfree laborers and slaves were excluded. Similar mechanisms could also be seen in the case of citizens in northern Italian communes of the medieval and Early Modern periods, patricians in city republics, or members of the Polish aristocratic republic. In the English parliament at Westminster, the parliamentary elites of the Lords and Commons were not operating in a democratic society or within a democratic political system with equal rights of participation. On the contrary, they successfully established "liberties," defined by the estates, and the opportunities for participation based on them. In this case, political control of the government and a separation of powers in principle correlated with a distinct inequality of political influence, which would persist until the major electoral reforms of the 19th century. For a long time, England could not be further away from being a motherland of democratic equality, although the country developed a functioning parliamentary system of checks and balances based on this long-established *ancien régime*. From the late 18th century, the traditional understanding of "liberties" as an expression of organically developed privileges came up against the new concept of *liberté*, which was inspired by natural law and proved to be open to new notions of political and social equality. This opposition also influenced our understanding of the differences between England's Glorious Revolution of 1689 and the principles of the French Revolution from 1789 onwards.[1]

II. EQUALITY IN SOCIO-POLITICAL PRACTICE SINCE THE LATE 18th CENTURY

In the course of the 18th century, contemporary debates about the meaning and scope of equality initially began at the level of theoretical reflection. This was true in particular for the program of the Enlightenment in its different variations, which revolved around the principle of equality. Here equality was repeatedly cited as a central goal of education or expressed in the evocative image of a cosmopolitanism in which the whole world was considered home—a context in which a natural equality of all people could be claimed. But theoretical reflections were not the end of the matter: the pluricentric global revolutions beginning in the last third of the 18th century meant concrete efforts to achieve political or social equality in North America, France, and the Caribbean. One result of these attempts appeared in newly formulated fundamental documents such as the *Bill of Rights*, the *Declaration of Independence*, and the *Declaration of the Rights of Man and of the Citizen*, whose influence extended far beyond their original context.

The assumed universalism of the political and social movements in North America, France, and Haiti necessitated the claim to global validity—which inspired the civilizing mission of the American and French Revolutions. However, looking at these revolutions in practice, active participation was limited to a relatively small minority, especially in North America. In France, the various versions of the constitution since 1789 underlined how varied and controversial the understanding of equality could be. These versions reflected conflicts over the scope of *égalité* with regard to its validity, ranging from the concept of equal rights for all citizens, implemented in a new property system after 1790 and ultimately in the codification of the *Core Civil* as pushed through by Napoleon, via demands for political equality with corresponding provisions regarding the active and passive right to vote linked to personal taxation and equality of early-life conditions and opportunities, through to demands for full social equality. The latter resulted in new kinds of state intervention, for example in the context of price- and wage-capping, or in the right to work and housing. In contemporary controversies about the range of impact brought about by legal, political, and social equality, negotiations concerned not only distinctions between reform and revolution, or between political/constitutional demands and socio-revolutionary movements, but also the function of the state. In any case, the categories of social equality anticipated the concept of "welfare" as a new task of the state.

Ultimately, as early as 1800 people in the age of global revolutions were already being confronted with universalist promises that were turning into the reality of power constellations and interest-based politics. How European concepts of equality lost their credibility could be seen for instance in the story of the Haitian Revolution after 1800. In the summer of 1791, the elite of plantation owners and slaves had responded to the revolution in France and its promises of equality. The events in the Caribbean accelerated the abolition of slavery in France, which finally took place in February 1794 through the National Convention. Its reintroduction under Napoleon, who did not want to lose income from the lucrative colony or a strategically important base in the Caribbean, provoked renewed uprisings. After a bloody civil war and repelling further British and French attempts to intervene, Haiti gained independence in 1804.[2]

III. STRUGGLES FOR EQUALITY IN THE 19th CENTURY: FOUR CRITERIA

In the long 19th century, between the revolutions of the 18th century and World War I, four processes became pertinent to the historical development of concepts of equality, processes which we can only outline here.[3] *First*, the defining model of the nation state developed out of the new goal of congruence between territory, people, domestic order, and external security in the name of sovereignty and territorial integrity. Contemporary commentators linked the nation state with the aspiration to homogenize populations in light of the new criterion of the nation, and to level out traditional differences in estate, denomination, or region. The resulting promises of equality were based on the understanding of sovereignty of the people and on the tectonics of reciprocal rights and duties between citizens and the state. These rights and duties formed the basis of citizenship law, but also stood behind military service, tax liabilities and the right to vote, compulsory education and, since the last third of the 19th century, in new entitlements to the welfare state. However, the transformation from a society of estates to an industrial society not only meant leveling out traditional differences but also brought about new types of stratification. Modern labor movements criticized the growing gap between political and social expectations of equality and actual experiences of inequality. The great "social questions" of the 19th century, from mass pauperism in the early decades to the struggle to integrate the industrial workforce in the second half of the century, increasingly drew attention to the state as an agent that was implementing new notions of equality.[4]

Second, the tension between freedom and equality shaped many struggles between societies and state authorities in the chain of revolutions that took place between 1789 and the Paris Commune uprising in 1871. By questioning the conditions needed for a functioning democracy in Europe and the United States, the French politician and political theorist Alexis de Tocqueville focused on the fundamental tension between freedom and equality. Looking at the authoritarian system of Napoleon III in France, he showed how civil liberties could be suspended by a *de facto* authoritarian regime through a clever use of plebiscites and by appealing to equality as an element of the sovereignty of the people. In the United States, by contrast, a balance between freedom and equality seemed possible—based on decentralized political decision-making and democratic virtues that could be experienced in local associations and assemblies, in a free press, and in the mechanisms of "town-hall democracy." When Tocqueville's contemporary John Stuart Mill concentrated on the dangers of the possible tyranny of the majority in the 1850s and 1860s, this provided another illustration of the contemporary view of the aporias within the promise of equality.[5]

Third, the 1848 revolutions exemplified how widely implementations of political and social equality could differ. While France in 1848, after the end of the monarchy, was dominated by the cult of democratic male suffrage as evidence of a progressive republic and later by the debate about the scope of the social republic with its own promise of equality, for German liberals the primary political model was the constitutional monarchy, the establishment of a German nation state, and the protection of political liberties. The social republic as the vehicle of socio-revolutionary notions of equality played an important role for German liberals only as a bugbear.[6] Since the 1850s, alongside limits to the domestic impact of equality and programmatic controversies, new spatial limitations to European promises of equality also emerged—namely in the practice of global colonialism with its inherent asymmetries and racist hierarchies.

Fourth, from the last third of the 19th century on, people of the time ultimately encountered a paradoxical situation. International ties and "globalization before globalization" were being reflected in an increasing number of standards and norms. But these trends towards alignment went hand in hand with more and increasingly visible inequality. The global nature of commerce and communication created an important launchpad for communicating comparisons. Processes of alignment and comparability made real inequality in many areas visible and tangible in the first place, whether in debates about women's suffrage around 1900 or in the issue of the conditions of dependent wage labor in various regions around the world.

IV. OUTLOOK: EQUALITY IN THE EARLY 20th CENTURY

In the early 20th century, the world wars that began in 1914 and 1939/41 highlighted radical new experiences of equality through millions of military and civilian war victims. At the same time, during these wars inequality was exacerbated through exclusion, ethnic violence, displacement, and mass murder perpetrated against those excluded from the warring nation. Here, in a historical context too, wars continued to act as catalysts for leveling processes and the emergence of new inequalities.

At the end of World War I, processes of democratization as a gradual expansion of political and social participation took place against the backdrop of millions of victims on the battlefront and on the home front. These processes were thus not solely the result of successful "revolutions from below," but often reflected the demands of collective wartime mobilization on a completely new scale. It was no coincidence that the German concept of *Volksgemeinschaft* [people's community] emerged during World War I. In many societies after 1918, the extension of the franchise as a breakthrough towards mass democracy was a response to the delegitimization of traditional political regimes during the war.[7]

Equally, since 1917 the radicalized promises of equality in ideological extremism, among the Russian Bolsheviks, in Italian fascism, in German National Socialism, and in many other authoritarian variations, referred repeatedly to the experience of war. Again and again, this involved a confrontation with civil society and its alleged cover-up of inequality while promoting new concepts of community, with terror becoming an accepted means in their enforcement. The promise of equality for the community went hand in hand with unbridled violence against all those excluded from that community. In the age of extremes, the discrepancy between the promise of equality and the practice of inequality reached its apogee in practices of exclusion and destruction.

Domestic developments had a particular counterpart in international politics. From the pivotal year of 1917, new international ideas were provoking global expectations of equality, whether in US President Woodrow Wilson's notions of a "world democracy" or in Lenin's vision of a "world revolution." Such ideas, summarized in the concept of *self-determination*, had already started developing into instances of empowerment and starting points for freedom movements in various regions of the world during the world war, for example in Asian and African countries. Here the practice of European colonialism came under even more pressure to justify itself, because from 1920 there also existed an international body for the expression of inequality in the shape of the League of Nations.[8]

Since the early 20th century, however, a variety of contradictions has also emerged in the way that concepts of equality are applied to international relations. Early on, the notion of internal and external state sovereignty, which since the 17th century had given rise to a group of state actors of generally equal status in the so-called "Westphalian System," approved a principle of equilibrium in order to prevent individual actors from hegemonic expansion. But these five Great Powers of Europe—Britain, France, Russia, Prussia, and Austria—necessitated the inequality of members and non-members, demonstrated by the way in which European states treated their colonies, and also in the elimination of states such as Poland in the 18th century.

Although the promise of self-determination had existed as a global promise since World War I and, in its potential appeal to a universal principle, had acted as an impetus towards the self-empowerment of local interests, the contradictions of liberal internationalism

became obvious soon after 1918. While the victorious powers in 1918 supported statehood for Poles,
Czechs, Slovaks, and Southern Slavs in Europe, the
same did not apply to the Irish, Ukrainians, Arabs, or
to colonial societies in Africa and Asia. The continu-
ation of colonial regimes after 1918 also contributed
significantly to the crisis of the West's credibility—and
in many regions of the world this continues to have
an impact today. As a result, in the sphere of international politics, one attribute remained decisive that
also characterized many social developments since the
19th century, namely a strained relationship between
promises of equality and experiences of inequality that
influenced the credibility of laws, regimes, and actors
in a substantial way—and continues to do so today.[9]

Notes

1. Otto Dann, "Gleichheit" in Otto Brunner, Werner Conze,
   and Reinhart Koselleck (eds.), *Geschichtliche Grundbegriffe:
   Historisches Lexikon zur politisch-sozialen Sprache in
   Deutschland*, vol. 2 (Stuttgart: Klett-Cotta Verlag, 1975), pp.
   997–1046; Thomas Mergel, "Gleichheit und Ungleichheit als
   zeithistorisches und soziologisches Problem" in *Zeithistorische
   Forschungen/Studies in Contemporary History* 10 (2) (Potsdam,
   2013), pp. 307–20.

2. Laurent Dubois, *Avengers of the New Worl⟨: The Story of the Haitian Revolution* (Cambridge, MA: Harvard University Press, 2004).

3. Jörg Fisch, *Europa zwischen Wachstum un⟨ Gleichheit 1850–1914* (Stuttgart: Utb Gmbh, 2002), pp. 27–37.

4. Werner Conze, "Vom Pöbel zum Proletariat: Sozialgeschichtliche Voraussetzungen für den Sozialismus in Deutschland" in *Vierteljahrschrift für Sozial- un⟨ Wirtschaftsgeschichte* 41, 1954, pp. 333–364; Hartmut Kaelble, *In⟨ustrialisierung un⟨ soziale Ungleichheit* (Göttingen: Vandenhoeck & Ruprecht, 1983).

5. Jörn Leonhard, "Freedom and the Tensions Between Collective Values: A Historical Perspective on the 19th Century" in Corinne Michaela Flick (ed.) in *How Much Free⟨om Must We Forgo to be Free?* (Munich: Convoco! Editions, 2022), pp. 141–58.

6. Dieter Langewiesche, "Republik, konstitutionelle Monarchie und 'soziale Frage': Grundprobleme der deutschen Revolution von 1848/49" in *Historische Zeitschrift* 230 (1), 1980, pp. 529–48.

7. Jörn Leonhard, *Pan⟨ora's Box: A History of the First Worl⟨ War*, trans. Patrick Camiller (Cambridge, MA/London: The Belknap Press of Harvard University Press, 2018).

8. Jörn Leonhard, "1917–1920 and the Global Revolution of Rising Expectations" in Stefan Rinke and Michael Wildt (eds.), *Revolutions an⟨ Counter-Revolutions: 1917 an⟨ its Aftermath from a Global Perspective* (Frankfurt am Main: Campus Verlag, 2017), pp. 31–51.

9. Jörn Leonhard, *Der überfor⟨erte Frie⟨en: Versailles un⟨ ⟨ie Welt 1918-1923*, 2nd edn. (Munich: C.H. Beck, 2019), pp. 1254–77.

CHAPTER 5

JUSTICE OR JUST IS? ECONOMICS AND INEQUALITY

RAJI JAYARAMAN

In the last two decades, the topic of inequality has entered the public discourse across a broad spectrum of issues with an urgency that is astonishing. To name but a few examples, the Occupy movement has called for more income equality, Black Lives Matter protesters have demanded racial equality, women's advocates have rallied behind causes as varied as equal pay and reproductive rights, and environmental activists have advocated for climate justice.

Surprisingly, economists are not front and center of this discussion. I say "surprisingly" because economists are supposed to be the experts on inequality: they measure and study it. I think the reason why economists have not played a more central role in this discussion is that the protesters in today's mass demonstrations are not just pointing out the existence of inequality, they are saying "inequality is unjust." With a few notable exceptions, however, today's empirical economists don't talk about justice. I fear that if economists don't incorporate justice into their analysis, they risk losing relevance.

Why don't applied economists, who deal with data and policy design, speak of justice in a meaningful way? I think it boils down to four fundamental axioms that will be familiar to every economist. First, allocations must be efficient. Second, evidence must be data-driven. Third, policies should be forward-looking. Fourth, choices are made "at the margin." As I explain below, I believe that these are very useful axioms. I also think, however, that they make it very hard for empirical economists who study inequality to effectively participate in the current debate on justice. In what follows, I explain why, using the four examples of protest movements to illustrate the crux of the problem.

To understand how the first axiom gets in the way, it is useful to start with a definition. In economics, an allocation is said to be efficient if there is no other allocation in which some other individual is better off and no individual is worse off. To understand what this means, consider a simple microeconomics 101 example. Suppose I have $10 that can be allocated between two people, Asha and Madhavi. One possible allocation is that Asha gets $4 and Madhavi gets $5. This allocation is not Pareto efficient because I've left money on the table: I could give Asha one more dollar and make her better off without making Madhavi worse off. You can see from this example why insisting on allocative efficiency is important: society as a whole is better off when we don't leave money on the table. A 5-5 allocation, which happens to be equal, is Pareto efficient. I have left no money on the table; from here, I can't reallocate this money to make one individual better off without making the other one worse off.

Now consider a different allocation, where Asha gets $9 and Madhavi gets $1. This 9-1 allocation is very unequal, but it is also efficient. In other words, there is no obvious efficiency rationale for redistribution, and you can see from this the potential tension between redistribution and efficiency. What does economists' focus on allocative efficiency mean for the current debate on inequality? We live in a world in which wealth and income are very unequally distributed: the bottom 55 percent of the world's population owns roughly 1 percent of the world's wealth, while the top 1 percent of the population owns 45 percent.[1] This seems patently unjust, but because it's not necessarily inefficient economists can look at this allocation and fail to share the same outrage as, say, the protesters from the Occupy movement.

Economists' focus on allocative efficiency can make them blind to injustice, and that's a serious problem. But what they do is still important to understanding inequality. For one thing, they carefully document its existence. The public probably wouldn't even know that global wealth was so unequally distributed if economists hadn't done the painstaking work of gathering the data and crunching the numbers.

In fact, thanks to the second axiom of empirical economics, they do even more than that. They use data-driven evidence to understand what drives inequality and figure out how to address it. To illustrate this, consider a second example: the gender pay gap. In most wealthy countries, women earn substantially less than men do. In the US, women earn just over 80 cents on each dollar that men make.[2] This pay gap varies from country to country, but it is always there.[3] Consequently, "equal pay for equal work" has served as a rallying cry for the gender equality movement the world over.

Economists rightly point out that this demand is too simplistic, because its implicit premise is that the only difference between men and women is their sex. That is simply not true. Men and women differ on all sorts of dimensions including (but not limited to) education, occupation, childbearing, and industry. Once you take these types of differences into consideration, at least in rich countries, you can account for most of the gender pay gap.

Suppose, hypothetically, that there is a 20-cent pay gap and that gender differences in education account for 5 cents of these 20 cents; occupation for another 4 cents; and childbearing for the remaining 11 cents. This is a data-driven exercise which allows one to understand where the gender pay gap is coming from. It's useful because once you understand where it is coming from, you can go about remedying opportunity gaps.

If, for example, education is one driver of the gender pay gap, then a potential policy intervention may be to motivate girls to study science by exposing them to its wonders at an early age or building their confidence in math. If women are choosing less remunerative occupations, you may want to incentivize them to become (say) programmers by investing in their computer skills or having role models in the tech sector. If there seems to be a "childbearing penalty," you could help mothers balance work and kids by allowing for remote working or subsidizing childcare. Economists study the effectiveness of these policies, and myriad others, aimed at fostering equity and reducing inequality.

In this way, by using data and analysis, economists can, and do, help to address inequities that equal pay protesters want remedied. The nuance and rigor that economists bring to bear are valuable, perhaps even indispensable. But, as you may have noticed from my example, there's a catch. Because empirical economists use data analytics, they focus on remedying inequality along measurable dimensions, such as education, occupations, or parenthood in my example.

The trouble is that not everything that is valuable is measurable. Going back to the gender pay gap example, what empirical economists are poorly equipped to discuss are things like social expectations regarding what women should or shouldn't do; perceptions regarding what women are or are not capable of doing; or values and the worth of activities of men and women. These things are all important, but because they are hard to measure, they don't figure in a lot of data-driven economic analyses.

This means that, although economists have important insights regarding how to address gender inequality, protesters demanding gender equality aren't necessarily impressed. They are asking for something different, something more: they are railing against institutions which they believe have built a system that has denied them equality and justice for centuries.

This leads us to the big blind spot in economic analysis, which is that we don't have a compelling framework for addressing historical injustice. A major reason for this is the third economic axiom: policies must be forward-looking. To illustrate why this is problematic, consider a third example. We live in a world with massive inequality across nations: rich countries have per capita GDPs that are anywhere between 50 to 100 times higher than that of the poorest countries.[4] The latter tend to be concentrated in Sub-Saharan Africa, but there are some exceptions. One is Haiti.

Why is Haiti so poor compared to its neighbors like Cuba, Jamaica, or even the Dominican Republic, which you might expect to be similar to Haiti given that they share the same island? Most economists will say, "Haiti is poor because it has weak institutions."[5] Haiti and the Dominican Republic may be similar in many respects but, they will say, Haiti has weak institutions that are based on extractive development rather than inclusive growth, whereas the Dominican Republic has much stronger institutions. For economists, the wealth of nations is built on strong institutions. In Haiti's case this would involve greater political stability and a different set of property rights. This is entirely reasonable: present-day institutions are undoubtedly important for economic development.

But there's another part to Haiti's economic development story that economists don't dwell on. Following Haiti's successful 1791 slave revolt, France demanded that Haiti's emancipated slaves pay their former enslavers 150 million francs. Economists estimate that over the next century and a half, these reparations ended up costing Haiti billions of dollars. During this time, Haiti went from being the richest country to the poorest country in the Americas.[6]

As a human being this seems terribly unjust. You can't help thinking, "Surely we owe it to Haiti to right this wrong." This view is not broadly shared among economists because, in economics, policy decisions must be forward-looking. Past sins may explain how we ended up where we are today but, from the economist's perspective, today's decisions should be based on today's payoffs and tomorrow's payoffs; historical injustice doesn't matter for what we do next. Economists would look at pictures of Black Lives

Matter demonstrators dumping a statue of the Bristol slave trader, Edward Colston, into the harbor and say, "Why are you throwing away a perfectly good piece of bronze?"

This willful ignorance of historical injustice limits economists' ability to make policy recommendations that resonate with public concerns expressed in many of today's social justice movements. This also follows from the fourth axiom: economic choices are made at the margin. Consider a final example to illustrate this: climate change. Especially in the last couple of years populations in North America, Europe, and Australia have witnessed some dramatic consequences of climate change, including wildfires and heatwaves. As horrific as these events have been, developing countries are really the ones facing the brunt of climate change. Populations in the Global South, which are poor to begin with, are experiencing severe droughts, floods, storms, and rises in sea levels that pose an existential threat to the lives of hundreds of millions.

Action is urgently needed, so it is only fitting that world leaders should congregate at climate summits, year after year, to find some way to keep global temperature rises in check. However, each time they meet they seem to hit a brick wall. Why is that?

Consider CO_2, which is a major contributor to global warming. If you look at CO_2 emissions today, Europe, the US, and Asia, including China and India, are the regions adding the most CO_2 to the atmosphere.[7] "At the margin," they are the largest contributors to global warming. Therefore, to combat climate change, Europe and the US must do their part to reduce emissions, but so must China and India. This economic insight is spot on: India and China are major contributors to climate change today and, because their economies are growing, they will be the largest contributors to climate change in the future. If they don't curb their emissions, the planet is doomed.

The trouble is that curbing emissions is a costly endeavor (although doing nothing is also untenable). Countries like China and India are quick to point out that climate change is a function of the stock of carbon in the atmosphere, and Europe and the US are responsible for most of this stock. Over the last 200 years, their economies grew at rates that were unprecedented in human history.[8] This growth was fed by fossil fuels, the planet has paid the price, and the Global South has borne the brunt. Is it just to ask the poorest countries to pay the cost of this folly?

That's what Greta Thunberg means when she says, "We can't call for climate justice while advocating for policies that exclude aspects of equity and historic emissions."[9] Her camp is calling for justice that considers the long arc of history while the other camp, guided by economic thinking, wants to focus on how to curb incremental contributions to pollution. Yet again, we find ourselves at an impasse.

It would be remiss of me not to mention that the empirical economists have made incredible contributions to the study of inequality. Whether they recognize it or not, the social justice movements sweeping the world today have relied heavily on economic insights. Thomas Piketty's work has laid the foundation for the global debate on income inequality.[10] The work of Abhijit Banerjee and Esther Duflo has lent texture to the lives of the poor and offered thoughtful solutions to the problems people face in countries like Haiti.[11] Claudia Goldin's work on gender equity has forced us to understand the intricacies of women and work.[12] Nick Stern's work was instrumental in bringing climate change into the public consciousness.[13] There are hundreds more. That these people are all economists is not an accident. Economics has an indispensable set of empirical tools that are, and must be, used to understand and address inequality. Social justice activists would do well to take advantage of the types of empirical insights, nuance, and pragmatic solutions that economics has to offer.

A fundamental problem, however, is that applied economics lacks a compelling way to think about justice. This is not to say that they don't think about the question of distributive justice at all. They do.[14] But dominant methods used to think about it are guided by utilitarianism and its descendants. Alternative ethical frameworks or questions of morality, which lie at the heart of justice, rarely figure in our empirical analyses. Unless applied economists (like me) find a way to incorporate justice into our otherwise remarkable empirical toolkit, we risk losing our relevance in the eyes of a public hungry for justice.

Notes

1. Credit Suisse Research Institute, "Global Wealth Report 2022," https://www.credit-suisse.com/about-us/en/reports-research/global-wealth-report.html (accessed October 13, 2022).

2. United States Census Bureau, "Equal Pay Day," Press Release Number CB22-SFS.33, March 15, 2022, https://www.census.gov/newsroom/stories/equal-pay-day.html (accessed October 13, 2022).

3. For differences within the EU see for example: European Commission, "The gender pay gap situation in the EU," https://ec.europa.eu/info/policies/

justice-and-fundamental-rights/gender-equality/equal-pay/
gender-pay-gap-situation-eu (accessed October 13, 2022).

4. Our World in Data, "Life expectancy vs. GDP per capita,
2018," https://ourworldindata.org/grapher/life-expectancy-
vs-gdp-per-capita (accessed October 13, 2022).

5. See for example: Daron Acemoğlu and James Robinson,
"Why is Haiti so poor?, Why Nations Fail Blog," April 3,
2012, http://whynationsfail.com/blog/2012/4/3/why-is-
haiti-so-poor.html (accessed October 13, 2022).

6. *New York Times*, "Haiti 'Ransom' Project," https://www.
nytimes.com/spotlight/haiti (accessed October 13, 2022).

7. Annual CO_2 emissions (fossil fuel and industry emission) by
world region, https://ourworldindata.org/grapher/annual-
co-emissions-by-region?time=1926..latest (accessed October
13, 2022).

8. Our World in Data, "GDP per Capita 1820 to 2018," https://
ourworldindata.org/grapher/gdp-per-capita-maddison-2020
(accessed October 13, 2022).

9. Greta Thunberg, Twitter, May 5, 2021, https://twitter.
com/gretathunberg/status/1389990642907066371 (accessed
October 13, 2022).

10. Thomas Piketty, *Capital in the Twenty-First Century*
(Cambridge, MA: Harvard University Press, 2014).

11. Abhijit V. Banerjee and Esther Duflo, *Poor Economics* (New
York: PublicAffairs, 2012).

12. Claudia Goldin, *Career & Family: Women's Century-Long
Journey Towar*￼ *Equity* (Princeton: Princeton University
Press, 2021).

13. Nicholas Stern, *The Economics of Climate Change: The Stern
Review* (Cambridge: Cambridge University Press, 2007).

14. See for example Amartya Sen, *The I*￼*ea of Justice* (Cambridge,
MA: Harvard University Press, 2011).

CHAPTER 6

ROMANTIC LOVE AND
INTERGENERATIONAL MOBILITY

KAI A. KONRAD

On December 10, 1936, Edward VIII renounced a kingdom to marry Wallis Simpson. Marriage to Wallis Simpson and his role as the British king were considered incompatible. We might say that Edward VIII valued his emotional happiness in a relationship more than royal titles, honors, and wealth. Together with Kjell Erik Lommerud, I have called this happiness in a relationship "love rent,"[1] clearly a very valuable commodity, since Edward VIII swapped a kingdom for it. People who are very much in love can make great sacrifices for their emotional happiness. But it doesn't always work out: there are certainly many cases when two people meet and fall in love, and the economic or social differences prove too great. Such examples provide good material for novels and plays—Jane Austen's *Pride and Prejudice* is one illustration. In the economic theory of marriage this notion is firmly established: from an economic point of view, a marriage typically means sharing a life, as well as one's economic affairs. In a marriage, the wealthier spouse shares much of the difference in wealth or income with the less wealthy person. This makes the wealth of a potential spouse one of the relevant criteria upon which decisions are made.

In the economic literature, many articles on marriage decisions support the importance of economic and social differences when deciding who to marry. For example, Michael Peters and Aloysius Siow describe how parents can improve their children's attractiveness as partners on the marriage market by investing in their human capital.[2] Similarly, in their observations Murat Iyigun and Randall Walsh assume that better education or more human capital improve a person's chances on the marriage market.[3] Overall, the role of economic attractiveness as one of the relevant criteria on the marriage market is an important starting point for theoretical investigations into the economic theory of such markets: economic wealth and social status can be counted alongside other characteristics that make a person more or less attractive as a potential partner.

Economic asymmetries can thus create obstacles for couples entering into a partnership for life. Lommerud and I argue that this also poses a problem that is relevant for economists from an efficiency point of view: if a marriage based on a love match fails due to economic differences, from society's point of view the emotional gratification that would arise from such a relationship is lost. The redistribution effects with and without marriage, on the other hand, are neutral in terms of welfare theory, because the marriage of a wealthy person to a poor person does not destroy wealth, it only redistributes it. These losses are less common in more egalitarian societies: wide economic gaps between lovers are rare in a highly egalitarian society.[4]

The problem of the failure of marriages based on a love match can basically be solved in two different ways. You can reduce inequality itself, or you can prevent economically unequal people from ever meeting one another and falling in love. If King Edward VIII and Wallis Simpson had never met, he would probably have met and married a nice person befitting his status, even if his love for her had been much less.

In fact, many societies do a great deal to ensure that the children of each social class preferably live, fall in love, and marry among their own kind. Marco van Leeuwen and Ineke Maas describe the extent and causes of "endogamy" or "homogamy" as class-conscious marriage is often called: you have to be acquainted in order to fall in love and later marry. Among the various contact options, the authors cite school and work, but also the area where people live, the Internet, and the family's social network. They describe past and present institutions where young people come into contact with each other. These institutions have a clear steering role. Many institutions encourage endogamy. School and work are two institutions that genuinely pursue primary goals other than the provision of partners, and a public, classless school system can tend to counteract endogamy. But here, too, there is a clear steering role through the differentiation of types of school into public schools and expensive, elite private schools.[5]

Among other parameters van Leeuwen and Maas generally include the probability of meeting across class and status boundaries, the search radius on the marriage market, and the degree of parental influence. Social norms and traditions, the social importance and acceptance of romantic feelings ("romantic love"), and the degree of young marriageable persons' economic independence from their families may also play a role.[6] Considering the various theories and reasons for endogamy leads Toft and Jarness to the thesis "that the cultural upper class will be comparatively more likely than the other upper-class fractions to have a partner in the same class fraction."[7] Equally, the tendency may be more pronounced among members of the upper classes if they're not "social climbers" but rather their antecedents already belonged to this class.[8] Empirical results show that a large section of the upper classes find marriage partners across class boundaries, but that the probability of an upper-class partnership is significantly higher than the probability of purely "random selection." Endogamy across cultural commonalities is even more pronounced than endogamy across economic commonalities—a result that fits well with the notion that cultural commonalities foster shared everyday pursuits.

The question of endogamy is of great importance to the overall theme of this book. Jens Beckert refers to the role of the dynastic family as one of the institutions favoring the perpetuation of great wealth.[9] He refers to the role of inheritance and how it is approached institutionally and fiscally. Marriage presents a key challenge to the intergenerational persistence of wealth within dynasties. The choice of partner could potentially lead to a diffusion of wealth. Beckert cites various sources as evidence of endogamy among the children of wealthy families. For example, Sander Wagner, Diederik Boertien, and Mette Gørtz use empirical data from Denmark to examine the importance of the parental wealth of children of marriageable age in their choice of partner.[10] They find the marriage probabilities of children from similarly wealthy families are significantly higher than those of a random pairing. This finding is more pronounced among the richest percentiles. And the tendency has increased over time. John Ermisch, Marco Francesconi, and Thomas Siedler also use empirical data from Germany and the United Kingdom to show that marriage between equals plays an important role in maintaining low economic intergenerational mobility, i.e. in the perpetuation of existing inequality between family dynasties.[11]

Marriage across income and wealth classes might be an important force in leveling educational and career opportunities and counteracting the increasing concentration of wealth within just a few family dynasties. In terms of social and economic policy, we might conclude that anyone whose primary goal is striving for more equality of wealth would have to entertain the idea of declaring war on the institutions that promote endogamy.

A rigid, integrated school system discourages endogamy. Equally, trends and movements that inspire young people from all classes are breaking down rigid boundaries between the social classes. Decades ago, in the collective Campaign against Nuclear Power in Gorleben and Wackersdorf, young opponents of the nuclear industry met, formed alliances, kissed, and fell in love across the social divide. The same happened in the peace movement during the "struggle" against the NATO Double-Track Decision or when attending festivals like Woodstock. In a long-forgotten television documentary, an interviewee and former participant in peace demonstrations put it much the same way, and in a manner we would now regard as completely politically incorrect: "...the girls in the peace movement were prettier than the students in the RCDS [Christian Democrat Students' League]." Today's growing movements such as "Fridays for Future" and "Extinction Rebellion" also have the potential to create relationships across boundaries of social class. Experiences such as "supergluing yourself and a group of friends to the freeway" create mutual solidarity and personal connections—and not just a literal connection with the road.

One thing is clear: it is possible to influence whether young people can meet each other across class boundaries. A more important question is, should the state intervene? For anyone whose primary goal is to bring about equal opportunities or even equality of outcome in the distribution of income and wealth this an important starting point. Possible political measures include an educational policy that gives all children largely the same opportunities at school and in their studies, prevents children in educational institutions from being streamed according to their origin and their parents' wealth and level of education, and restricts opportunities for wealthy or well-educated parents to patronize forms of education beyond what is available to the general public. The same applies to university courses and other training opportunities. The state can intervene in the way young people spend their free time and prevent them from being divided into groups along the lines of their parents' status. Large transfers of assets within the family are an obstacle to marriage across class boundaries. The state can impose higher taxes on the transfer of assets in the context of inheritance and thus increase intergenerational equality of distribution too. When young people meet in their neighborhood, mixed housing projects are more conducive to the possibility of "mixed" marriages than housing projects that reflect a society's class divides.

However, all these policies need to be considered and weighed carefully against each other, even if great store is placed on achieving wealth equality. Such interventions have considerable secondary effects and side effects and represent options for forms of state intervention that might not fit with a free society. Among the measures discussed, inheritance tax law is probably the political intervention that is most appropriate for a free society.

Notes

1. Kai A. Konrad and Kjell Erik Lommerud, "Love and Taxes – And Matching Institutions" in *The Canadian Journal of Economics* 43 (3), 2010, pp. 919–40.

2. Michael Peters and Aloysius Siow, "Competing Premarital Investments" in *Journal of Political Economy* 110 (3), 2002, pp. 592–608.

3. Murat Iyigun and Randall P. Walsh, "Building the Family Nest: Premarital Investments, Marriage Markets, and Spousal Allocations" in *The Review of Economic Studies* 74 (2), 2007, pp. 507–35.

4. Konrad and Lommerud, "Love and Taxes."

5. Marco H. D. van Leeuwen and Ineke Maas, "Endogamy and Social Class in History: An Overview" in *International Review of Social History* 50, 2005, pp. 1–23.

6. Ibid.

7. Maren Toft and Vegard Jarness, "Upper-class Romance: Homogamy at the Apex of the Class Structure" in *European Societies* 23 (1), 2021, pp. 71–97; here p. 77.

8. Toft and Jarness, "Upper-class Romance," p. 78.

9. Jens Beckert, "Durable Wealth: Institutions, Mechanisms, and Practices of Wealth Perpetuation" in *Annual Review of Sociology* 48, 2022, pp. 233–55.

10. Sander Wagner, Diederik Boertien, and Mette Gørtz, "The Wealth of Parents: Trends Over Time in Assortative Mating Based on Parental Wealth" in *Demography* 57 (5), 2020, pp. 1809–31.

11. John Ermisch, Marco Francesconi, and Thomas Siedler, "Intergenerational Mobility and Marital Sorting" in *The Economic Journal* 116 (513), 2006, pp. 659–79.

CHAPTER 7

SOCIAL MOBILITY
AND MERITOCRACY

CLEMENS FUEST

I. THE ROLE OF SOCIAL MOBILITY IN THE DEBATE ABOUT THE DISTRIBUTION OF WEALTH AND INCOME

Social mobility plays a central role in debates about distribution. An unequal distribution of income and wealth at a given point in time is part of a free market economy. For most people, inequality is more likely to be acceptable if it is a reflection of individual performance and, in principle, everyone has the opportunity of advancement and prosperity through performance. Whether social structures are meritocratic to this effect is often measured by the extent of social mobility. Typically, social mobility is determined by the extent to which people whose parents have low incomes or wealth advance into more affluent groups, and vice versa. Social mobility can also exist in terms of education, status, and other variables. Social mobility is often defined as relative mobility, which means that increasing opportunities for social advancement are necessarily associated with an increasing probability of social decline in society.

Stagnating or declining social mobility is often seen as an indication that social structures are hierarchical and unfairly grant privileges to certain groups or prevent the rightful advancement of others. In fact, drawing conclusions about prevailing social conditions from the degree of observed social mobility is not as straightforward. This essay addresses the question of the connection between social mobility and society's rules of engagement when it comes to social advancement and social decline. The analysis focuses on showing that even declining social mobility is not necessarily a symptom of a departure from meritocratic structures. Indeed, a temporary decrease in social mobility may arise as part of a normal process of development as societies shift towards more meritocratic structures with wider opportunities for advancement. This is because over the course of this process of development there may be an increase in social mobility that exceeds the long-term level of mobility in a perfectly meritocratic society. Using a simplified economic model of social mobility, the following analysis shows that when societies with hierarchical or aristocratic structures transition towards meritocratic structures, an initial increase followed by a decrease in social mobility can be expected, based on certain premises.

This raises the question of whether such developments can also be observed empirically. The empirical analysis of changes in social mobility requires data that stretches over very long time periods. At the same time, social mobility is not only influenced by the role meritocratic aspects play in gaining access to wealth and social advancement. Data for the period 1840 to 1910 does show that social mobility in the United States increased initially, peaked in the period after the Civil War, and then decreased again. If we assume that meritocratic structures became more significant in American society during this period, then the observed development of social mobility could be explained using the arguments developed in this essay.

II. A SIMPLE MODEL OF SOCIAL MOBILITY

Let us consider a model economy with population size N, whose members differ in their productivity. In each cohort, $X < N$ are highly productive and $N - X$ are less productive individuals. Highly productive individuals produce Z units of output, while less productive individuals produce $Y < Z$ units of output. Each cohort lives for one period of time. Each individual has one child who lives in the following period. The probability that the child of a highly productive individual also becomes highly productive is $0 < p < 1$, so that the child is less productive with a probability of $1 - p > 0$. The probability that the child of a less productive individual turns out to be highly productive is $0 < q < 1$. Here productivity is a characteristic a person is born with. The analysis thus abstracts from investments in education. The role of these and other assumptions on which the analysis is based will be discussed in more detail below.

What is the proportion of individuals in this society who have high or low productivity? X_t highly productive individuals live in period t, and their offspring pX_t are also highly productive. The $N - X_t$ less productive individuals in the same cohort have $q(N - X_t)$ highly productive children. So the number of highly productive individuals in period $t+1$ is as follows:

$$X_{t+1} = pX_t + q(N - X_t)$$

In a long-run stationary equilibrium, in which $X_{t+1} = X_t$ holds, the number of highly productive individuals evens out at the value:

$$X = \frac{qN}{1 - p + q}$$

Total economic production is the sum generated by X highly productive and $N - X$ less productive individuals:

$$XZ + (N - X)Y = \frac{qN}{1 - p + q}(Z - Y) + NY$$

This total economic production corresponds to the sum of incomes in each period. How do differences arise in this society? Suppose there are good and bad jobs. In the case of the good jobs, the pay is Z, which equals to the production or "performance" of a highly productive individual. In the case of the bad jobs, the pay is only Y. This does not say anything about who gets the good jobs and who gets the bad jobs and the pay that goes with them. That depends on the institutions in society.

II.1 MERITOCRACY

In a meritocratic society, highly productive individuals get the well-paid jobs, while others get the bad jobs. Since the children of highly productive individuals are not necessarily highly productive themselves, social mobility takes place. In the following section, we will measure social mobility by the number of people who have good jobs even though their parents had bad jobs. In a meritocracy, in each cohort X people have well-paid jobs, but $(1 - p)X$ of these people have children who are not highly productive. Because this is a meritocracy, these children experience social decline and end up in bad jobs, while just as many children of low-productive parents are highly productive and move up accordingly. So social mobility in a meritocracy is given by:

$$s^M = \left[\frac{qN}{(1 - p + q)}\right](1 - p) \tag{1}$$

The greater the probability that less productive people will have highly productive children, the greater the social mobility, because an increasing q-value simply means that more people are moving up the ladder. Since the proportion of highly productive individuals in the population is higher when q is bigger, overall prosperity increases as well. If the probability that highly productive people will have highly productive children (p) increases, then the consequences for social mobility are characterized by two opposing effects. On the one hand, this also increases the number of highly productive individuals in the population and with them the number of good jobs. On the other hand, the proportion of social decliners falls because more good jobs now go to individuals whose parents already had good jobs. On balance, social mobility decreases.

II.2 ARISTOCRACY

The opposite of a meritocracy would be a society in which access to wealth, represented here by good jobs, is not determined by performance but, for example, by birth, by membership of the aristocracy. If only the aristocracy has access to good jobs, social mobility is zero. Typically, however, societies with a privileged class are characterized by the fact that at the same time opportunities for advancement exist for highly productive people who are not born into the aristocracy. But the number of people who can move up is limited because some of the positions with high incomes are held by aristocrats.

In the model considered here, this can be illustrated as follows. Suppose the aristocratic "elite" consists of a given number of persons E. Their children automatically belong to the aristocracy. The aristocracy is no more or less talented than the rest of the population. So the proportion of highly productive individuals in the aristocracy is EX/N. Every member of the aristocracy automatically gets a good job, regardless of their own productivity. So for the rest of the population, $X - E$ well-paid positions are available. These positions are assigned to highly productive but non-aristocratic individuals at random. The probability of a highly productive non-aristocratic individual getting such a job is given by:

$$\frac{X - E}{X - E(X/N)} < 1$$

It follows that the aristocrats with low productivity obtain the income of highly productive non-aristocrats who do not manage to get a good job.

What is the extent of social mobility in an aristocracy? Of the $X - E$ persons who have a good job but do not belong to the aristocracy, a proportion $(1 - p)$ will have children who do not get good jobs and are consequently replaced by social achievers. So social mobility is given by $(X - E)(1 - p)$. Inserting the value for X into the long-run equilibrium condition leads to:

$$s^A = \left[\frac{qN}{(1 - p + q)} - E\right](1 - p) \tag{2}$$

Comparison with equation (1) shows that social mobility is lower in the aristocracy. That's no surprise. The larger the group of aristocrats, the less space there is for highly productive non-aristocrats to advance. If we compare established aristocratic societies with established meritocratic societies, then from the perspective of this model, which abstracts from other differences, meritocratic societies should exhibit permanently greater social mobility. However, this says nothing about how social mobility develops in the process of transition from one form of society to another.

II.3 TRANSITION FROM ARISTOCRACY TO MERITOCRACY

Now let's suppose that an aristocratic society is radically transformed from one period of time to the next, and the rules about access to good jobs switch to meritocratic principles. As a result, aristocrats lose their privileged access, and good jobs go exclusively to highly productive individuals. Among the aristocrats, the number of parents whose children are no longer able to get good, highly paid jobs is given by:

$$\frac{E}{N}\left(X(1-p) + (N-X)(1-q)\right)$$

Among the children of non-aristocrats who had well-paid jobs in the last period of time, the number of those who do not get a well-paid job is:

$$(X-E)(1-p)$$

Accordingly, the number of those who get a good job while their parents didn't is given by:

$$\frac{E}{N}\left(X(1-p) + (N-X)(1-q)\right) + (X-E)(1-p)$$

The extent of social mobility during the transition from aristocracy to meritocracy can thus be expressed as:

$$s^T = \left[\frac{qN}{(1-p+q)}\right](1-p) + \left[1-\frac{X}{N}\right]E(p-q) \tag{3}$$

Comparing equations (3) and (1) shows that social mobility in this phase of transition is higher than during the established state of meritocracy, if and only if $p>q$ holds, that is the second term on the right-hand side of (3) is positive. If this condition is met, the increase in social mobility in the phase of transition from aristocratic to meritocratic structures is followed by a decrease in social mobility. Here, however, this decrease is not a symptom of a return to the aristocracy with its privileges that are not based on performance or productivity. It rather indicates the establishment of meritocracy. This means that the empirical observation of a decrease in social mobility over a certain period of time does not necessarily mean that meritocratic structures are diminished but may be a consequence of their establishment.

These considerations thus lead to the empirical prediction that in processes of social change towards more meritocratic structures social mobility first increases and then decreases again, but without returning to the low level that preceded the change. However, this only applies if the correlation of abilities between parents and their children is positive in the sense that highly productive parents are more likely to have highly productive children. This seems plausible, especially when one considers that abilities are not solely and probably not even primarily determined by genetic make-up, but rather by upbringing and education, on which parents have a very great influence. Whether the transfer of human capital from parents to children as such should be seen as reflecting meritocracy is another issue.

As mentioned at the beginning, there is a lack of data for sufficiently long periods of change in social mobility to empirically verify this hypothesis.

Social Mobility in the USA 1840-1910

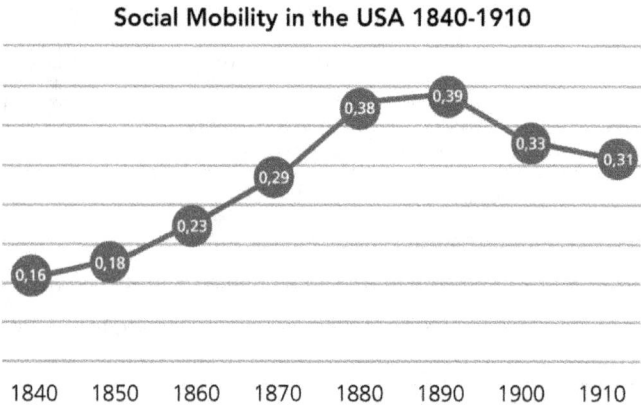

Source: *Zachary War*, *Own calculations. Here, 1-k is chosen as the measure of social mobility, where k is the correlation in the status of fathers an* sons as calculate* by War*. See War* (2022), p. 38.*

However, in a recent study in economic history, Zachary Ward analyzes changes in social mobility in the US in the 19th and 20th centuries and draws conclusions for the period between 1840 and 1910 that correspond to the development of social mobility we have elaborated theoretically here, provided we assume that US society has developed more in the direction of meritocratic structures in the period in question.

III. OUTLOOK

Opportunities for advancement for wide strata of the population are part of a free market economy. When performance offers access to advancement opportunities, this strengthens performance incentives. This is an important driver for the creation of wealth. At the same time, productivity is determined to a large extent by human capital, which for the most part does not depend on one's own efforts and only partly on parental efforts. To this extent, we can certainly ask whether meritocratic societies, in which performance determines advancement, are "fairer" than other forms of society in terms of equal opportunities. There is also the problem, as described by Michael Young in his seminal 1958 work on meritocracy, that those who decline or are "lower class" in meritocratic socie-ties also "deserve" it. This creates a great potential for conflict. In this respect, it is probably less regrettable than often expected that pure meritocratic societies are an extreme theoretical case from which real-life circumstances differ significantly.

At the same time, the growing importance of meri-tocratic structures associated with the spread of free market democracies is certainly an important factor for the economic success of this social system. However, the success of free market democracies is also increas-ingly measured by the fact that the economic prosperity they generate reaches large sections of the population.

Social mobility is an important prerequisite for this. It is therefore important to improve our under-standing of the connection between social mobility and the institutions in society.

Bibliography

Zachary Ward, "Intergenerational Mobility in American History: Accounting for Race and Measurement Error," *NBER Working Paper 29256* (Cambridge, MA: National Bureau of Economic Research, 2022).

Michael Young, *The Rise of the Meritocracy, 1870–2033: An Essay on Education and Equality* (London: Thames and Hudson, 1958).

CHAPTER 8

REVERSING POLARIZATION: HOW PEOPLE CAN FIND COMMON PURPOSE

PAUL COLLIER

The equality of opportunity between generations is a very fine common purpose for a society. I come from the society of Britain, which has the lowest inter-generational mobility in the whole of the OECD. Sheffield, my hometown, is now the poorest city in the whole of England. And South Yorkshire, my region, was the heartland of the Brexit vote. The Brexit vote can be predicted very well in terms of how well a region has done. My home region used to be prosperous but has collapsed.

The government has done research on what societal purposes people agree on in Britain, what their common ground is. Today, Britain is a very polarized society. There is only one thing everybody agrees on, regardless of party affiliation, regardless of whether they voted Brexit or Remain, regardless of class, regardless of income. The people of Britain agree that there is a big difference between the opportunities of children born to working-class parents in poor parts of the country, and those born to middle-class parents and brought up in rich parts of the country. Leveling up these big intergenerational inequalities is the only common purpose that Britain can find—but it is clearly worthwhile.

The following essay will proceed in three parts. First, we are going to look at communities and polities. Second, we will address the process of transition: how do we change from a disastrous society like Britain to one united around this common purpose of intergenerational mobility? What process can bring people together? Finally, I want to discuss the situation in Germany, which I believe is at a pivotal moment.

Let me start with communities and polities. In order to understand communities, we need to take a brief look at the latest research on evolutionary biology. The current world leader in this field is Joseph Henrich, head of the department of human evolutionary biology at Harvard. His essential argument is that unfortunately humans have evolved to be less than saints. We're a mammal, and most mammals are greedy, selfish, and lazy. Nevertheless, we are a very unusual one. For a start, we have evolved over the last 200,000 years to be remarkably prosocial. We work in groups, and there's a very good reason for that. When we came down from the trees onto the African savanna, we didn't have fur, armor-plating, or scales, unlike other animals, nor did we have big claws. We were trying to stand upright to see above the grass, but we weren't very good at it because we were designed to move on four legs not two. We weren't very fast either. Yet we found ourselves in a desperately scary environment populated by mammoths and lions. The only way we could survive was to cooperate in big groups. These groups of around 150 individuals taught us mutuality. We learned to work together for common purposes and to trust each other. One hundred and fifty people is thought to be the maximum number of people that one can know (also known as the "Dunbar Constant"). By means of gossip within such a community, individuals can gradually build a reputation for being either reliable or unreliable. And with that incentive, one can build a reputation for being trustworthy. That's the evolutionary process that made humans unusually prosocial, leading to communities that trust each other and cooperate for common purposes. In addition to that, we turned out to be remarkably imaginative and creative. This is another feature in which we're a unique mammal. Take squirrels for comparison. Squirrels are very clever: they think ahead and save nuts for when it's cold and there's no food. But what squirrels don't seem to have done at any stage in their evolution is to imagine whether there is a better way of life than being a squirrel. If you want to understand the life of a squirrel 100,000 years ago, you just need look at one today. Their genetics and behavior remain unchanged. If, on the other hand, we want to understand the behavior of people 100,000 years ago, it's completely useless to look at people today.

How have we got from where we were 100,000 years ago, terrified about being chased by a lion or gored by some other mammal, to today? We managed to face this common challenge by being social, imaginative, and creative. That has driven us to ever more ambitious goals and purposes. Human beings can imagine things that are better than the situation we're in. Our tragedy is that it's much easier to imagine better things than to achieve them. That is the unique feature of the human condition, and it plunges us into a state known as radical uncertainty: we're always trying to achieve goals that we don't know how to achieve.

In modernity we live in big organizations, in communities of work and of place. Modernity is a world that goes beyond communities. It's a world of political entities and states. Polities have a very different dynamics from communities. As mentioned above, communities can comprise up to 150 individuals. They can't grow much beyond that because we can't know and trust everybody. Polities, however, can be big. Polities have emerged from scale economies and violence. They are militarized hierarchies in which a leader used his military power to build a polity. The big advantage of polities over communities is scale. Every economist will agree that scale is very useful. I spent much of my life working with the "bottom billion"—left-behind countries or regions within countries that are struggling to catch up with the rest of humankind. In recent years, many of them have been losing that struggle because although people work hard, they are desperately short of firms, the organizations that would enable them to reap economies of scale.

Polities are therefore useful because they enable the scale necessary to escape mass poverty. Communities on the other hand produce mutuality and trust. What we need is a combination of these features of community and polity. However, combining the two is very difficult. Almost every place in the world has both polities and communities, but few have managed to fuse them to their advantage. Most places I work on have instead fused the worst features of polities and communities. These are societies doomed to mass poverty because they can't do economies of scale in production, and their communities are fragmented with oppositional identities while no leader enjoys enough trust to pull them together.

How do we escape this situation? How can we transition away from a polarized society to one that comes together? I want to suggest three principles with practical examples. The first principle is that we need to fuse two very different sorts of knowledge. One is the generic knowledge of academics like myself. If you are looking for an informed strategy to guide a society, it's not a bad idea to listen to a specialist. But we should never leave these specialists in charge because academics often have little lived experience. We need to draw on their form of generic knowledge, but agency must lie with the people who have the necessary contextual knowledge of lived experience. For example, in my home region of Sheffield in South Yorkshire there's a remarkable process taking place of people coming together around a new common purpose: we want South Yorkshire to be a more prosperous place for our children. But to achieve that it is vital that local people have the agency, not the politicians in London. The politicians in London won't be able to save Sheffield because they know too little about the city. The UK has become the most centralized society in Europe. Agency must instead be more localized. German society is considerably more devolved by comparison. This fusion of generic and contextual knowledge is crucial.

This brings us to the second principle: subsidiarity. Subsidiarity is about who exactly should have agency for achieving a goal. And the answer is: the lowest level at which that goal is feasible to be achieved. Some goals can only be achieved with global cooperation. Peace in Europe has to be achieved only by the whole of Europe coming together. Other goals can be achieved at the level of the city.

The final principle is rapid learning. Given that we are faced with humanity's existential problem of trying to achieve goals that we don't know how to achieve, what should we do? We must learn rapidly, from others and from experiment. To experiment means to try different things and to track what is working. For example, Britain should have known that COVID was coming. After all, it had already happened in Italy. The British Civil Service, however, has a belief that it is the finest civil service in the world and so doesn't need to look at anything else. If it looks anywhere, it looks at America and congratulates itself on being better.

If we look at differences in life chances—the levels of intergenerational social inequality—Britain has the highest level of inequality of any country except for Peru. Denmark has the lowest degree of intergenerational inequality in the modern world. And the difference between Denmark and Britain is staggering. How do we get from Britain to Denmark? How do we escape such extreme polarization?

There are bottom-up processes and top-down processes. The great student of the bottom-up processes is the Harvard sociologist Robert Putnam. His magnum opus is a book called *The Upswing*. Bottom-up processes work in both directions. First, there are bottom-up processes that build hatreds. Here we need look no further than social media. Social media has produced teenagers obsessing about their curated selves. Girls in particular are terrified that their online selves are not sufficiently attractive. Suicide and depression rates among teenagers have skyrocketed. This is a tragedy that's entirely avoidable. But social media can have even worse effects: in 1992, Ethiopia was an extremely poor society, which for twenty years grew very fast, leading to great successes in reducing poverty and bringing society together. Then it fell into civil war. And what helped to ignite that civil war? Facebook, (now rebranded as Meta). Facebook developed algorithms designed by the most brilliant people in the world, whose purpose is to keep people on the platform: this is because Facebook's revenue source is ads. Frances Haugen, a very senior Facebook official turned whistleblower, testified under oath in the British Parliament that Facebook's algorithms were intentionally designed to feed people's extreme views. Across the US, there were many Ethiopian migrants from different ethnic groups, for example, the Oromo, the Amhara, the Tigrayans, etc. These groups wanted to stoke grievances against other groups living in their home regions. Even before Ethiopia got into civil war, appalling violence broke out in various regions as the majority ethnic group in each region, incited by emigrants in America, advocated ethnic cleansing. The ensuing violence displaced three million people within Ethiopia, and it was all driven by Facebook algorithms. The devastating evidence is that Facebook knew this was happening but allowed it to continue because it was profitable. This is an example of a bottom-up process that can build hatreds.

Fortunately, there are also bottom-up processes of kindness. Robert Putnam's wonderful book tells the story of the formation of the Rotary Club. The Rotary Club was founded by Paul Harris. Harris was from a small town in Iowa with a strong sense of community. When he migrated to boom-town Chicago, he got a good job and was doing well, but he was lonely because he missed that sense of community. In Chicago, he could only find a lot of successful individualists like himself. He thus decided to put out an advert in the paper, asking for others like him, those who were successful but lonely, to get together. Two hundred people showed up for the first meeting. There they all agreed that this new society's purpose would not be to discuss business deals, but to further community action in Chicago. Thus was born the Rotary Club, with the purpose of helping the less fortunate people of Chicago as its guiding principle. Ten years later, the club was so successful that it branched out to other towns in America. Today, the Rotary Club is an international organization with millions of people. Of course, the members of the Rotary Club are not saints. But they are much better than the greedy, lazy, selfish individualists who libertarians such as Liz Truss and Ayn Rand celebrate.

Let me give you one other example of kindness. Because my grandfather lived in a little village near Stuttgart, I'm often invited back to Stuttgart to speak. The business community in Stuttgart has come together impressively by establishing a norm to train the city's next generation of young people—not just the clever people who are going to become lawyers, but the people who just want a skilled job. I noticed that in Germany and in Switzerland firms don't brag about how many people they are training. If one firm chose to save money by not training the next generation of local youth, they'd feel ashamed about it. In Britain, on the other hand, the training of young people has completely collapsed since the apprentice system was dismantled. This is a major reason for the lack of social mobility in the UK. You either go to university and become a lawyer or some other lucrative profession, or your opportunities collapse. There is no middle ground of skill left in Britain. Trying to rebuild that is enormously difficult. Individual firms don't want to train because the cost is too high. That's the trap into which Britain has fallen.

What about the top-down processes? Top-down processes are interesting because there are two styles of leadership that are both evolutionarily stable and unique to humanity. In the animal world, there is only one stable form of leadership: the alpha male. There are many examples of modern political leaders who exhibit this alpha-male type of leadership by dominance. Until recently, one such leader was president of the United States of America. Today, we look closer to home and see in Putin an extreme alpha male. This dominance of a leader is characterized by bragging and exaggerated self-confidence. I have already suggested that humanity's radical uncertainty requires us to embrace rapid learning. Does Putin follow the principle of rapid learning? No! He's made the fundamental mistake of every dictator before him and surrounded himself by people who dare not tell him even the basic realities. By comparison, Ukraine's President Volodymyr Zelenskyy is a very different type of leader. This difference shows itself in their respective backgrounds. President Putin's background is the military intelligence and hierarchy from his time in the KGB. Zelenskyy's background, on the other hand, is comedy and entertainment, which makes him very good at communicating.

Along these lines I distinguish two types of leaders: commanders-in-chief and communicators-in-chief. When Putin invaded Ukraine, Ukraine desperately needed a communicator-in-chief like Zelenskyy who could speak to people and say, "Things have changed. We're going to have to learn rapidly." He established trustworthiness through a statement of self-sacrifice: "I am going to stay in Kyiv even though I'm target number one. I am willing to die in Kyiv because I believe in this country." After establishing credibility, he suggested a strategy: "If we fight against Putin, I can talk to leaders of other countries and shame their respective communities into helping us. But you must show solidarity of purpose. If you're a male of fighting age, I ask you to stay in Ukraine and fight. But I cannot tell you exactly what you need to do. I'm a comedian, not a soldier. Therefore, I'm going to devolve agency to local fighting groups. Join your militia in your town and work out yourselves how best to resist." That's a strategy of devolved agency, and it began to work. Zelenskyy is a brilliant communicator. Country after country, he appealed directly to the people of other nations to shame their leaders into action, leading to significant change. Zelenskyy is an example of the type of leaders we need for the 21st century. Zelenskyy brought Ukraine together under a common identity, uniting both Russian speakers and Ukrainian speakers to say, "We're all Ukrainians."

Finally, let me turn to what this implies for Germany. For a long time, Germany did not face up to its unavoidable role of leadership in Europe. Instead, it clung to the comfortable illusion that morally defensible choices such as reducing gross differences in life chances within Europe could be reconciled with the economics of convenience: dependence on cheap Russian gas and the vast Chinese market for German exports. As President Frank-Walter Steinmeier has now bravely recognized, Putin's invasion of Ukraine, and Chinese support for it, have decisively refuted that illusion. Germany will have to make substantial sacrifices to lead Europe into coming together around the common purpose of confronting aggression.

As in Ukraine, European leadership will need people with the moral decency to bring people together around a socially worthwhile purpose. They will need the communication skills to set that purpose as a common goal. And they will need the modesty to devolve agency to others, both to advisors and to local people—whose key advantage is that they are the experts in knowing the context of their locality. Fortunately, the signs are encouraging: the transformation masterminded by Chancellor Olaf Scholz and President Frank-Walter Steinmeier has been swift, courageous, and irreversible. I can only hope that British leaders learn from their example.

CHAPTER 9

GUARANTEED PROSPERITY?
THE GERMAN EXPERIENCE

WOLFGANG SCHÖN

Since the outbreak of the COVID-19 pandemic in early
2020 and on through the current energy and supply-
chain crisis, of which Russia's war against Ukraine is
just one albeit the main cause, Germany's social model
has been under considerable pressure. The lockdowns
of 2020 and 2021 have bankrupted many companies
and brought others to the brink, while the dramatic
increases in gas and electricity costs in 2022 have
caused profits to collapse again and prices to rise. The
increase in consumer prices is causing hardship to
those in lower income brackets in particular; the rise

in interest rates has shattered many people's dreams of owning a home. Germany is concerned about the danger of social decline affecting broad sections of the population, but also about the competitiveness of its economy. And Germany is not alone in this—most European countries face the specter of broad social and economic decline, and most European politicians have to cope with it.

In recent years, German politicians—beyond the change of government in 2021—have reacted with a variety of measures that share a common trait: they are designed to maintain the status quo for all citizens. COVID-19 subsidies and short-time working benefits, tax holidays, and gas-price caps are all connected by the idea of protecting citizens from the challenges of the time. Prosperity—this leads us to believe—is guaranteed, and what the free market cannot provide is considered to be the task of the state. And the state will always focus on equality when dealing with this task—the normative equality of citizens in their constitutional entitlement to a minimum level of social security, but also the very real inequality of the way each person is affected differently and fatefully by crises and catastrophes.

The policy of guaranteed prosperity draws, it seems, on three different sources. The first and most obvious justification for most measures is the notion that short-term shocks should not destroy long-term investments. Establishing a company, the effort involved in one's own education, and the creation of the individual's personal world (including one's own place of residence) take most people many years, perhaps even several generations; this "sunk investment" should not be wiped out by isolated and seemingly arbitrary shocks. That is why efforts are being made to preserve companies and jobs, mandating tax, rent, and loan payment holidays, and distributing social benefits to enable people to stay in their own homes. That seems good and right, but it only works if the crisis to be managed does indeed remain brief and isolated. The situation becomes more difficult if these crises last longer than expected or if crisis upon crisis ensues. How many crises have we experienced in Europe since the turn of the millennium alone? The seemingly endless series of disruptions ranges from the financial market crisis via the Euro crisis and the migration crisis to the COVID-19 crisis and the Ukraine crisis. And in the background has been the greatest challenge of all for decades—climate change—which is jeopardizing not only global prosperity but also the survival of large parts of humanity. However, the idea of being able to counter this permanent shift from one crisis to the next with ever new temporary assistance is not tenable, because it assumes a constant capacity on the part of the state, whose economic foundations are also being shaken by the very same crises. If the economy falters, so does the state, whose ability to act draws not only ideologically but also financially on conditions that it cannot itself guarantee.

The second line of reasoning is socio-psychological. Politicians and citizens seem to agree that Germany is a "rich country" whose normal situation is full employment, a growing gross national product, moderate interest rates (enough for savers, not too high for borrowers), and strong exports that promote prosperity. Large-scale confrontations caused by collapsing supply chains, energy costs that damage competition, falling foreign demand, sharply rising defense costs, etc. are not envisaged by this model. Prosperity is the norm; crisis is the exception. Politicians therefore see it as their duty to guarantee this prosperity, which has been established for decades and which the population assumes to be secure. Taking a step backwards is not part of the plan and is always perceived and declared by politicians to be a failure, even when, as in the case of the war in Ukraine, the main causes lie outside their sphere of influence. This perspective is structurally backward-looking. It reflects a kind of longstanding political discourse that always gives the best chances of winning elections to those who can maintain the status quo. As one German Chancellor said on the occasion of German reunification: "No one will be worse off than before—but many will be better off."[1] Advancement is always an option, decline is not. However, this also goes hand in hand with a structurally pessimistic worldview that sees the solution to economic and social problems in the preservation of established structures, and in which innovation is considered pointless as a way of stimulating welfare—even in terms of "creative destruction" (cf. Joseph Schumpeter).

Closely linked to this image of a policy aimed at preserving prosperity is a benevolent view of the situation of individuals in society, to whom one cannot attribute any personal blame for the impending loss of prosperity and whom one would therefore like to exempt from all negative consequences. Of course, it is true that neither the COVID-19 pandemic nor the war in Ukraine were started or encouraged by German society. In which case—so it seems—the negative consequences of these international developments are not to be offloaded onto the German people. This shows an understanding of statehood that no longer recognizes the kind of fate that is unfavorable to the individual. Since antiquity the tradition has been completely different: *casum sentit ꞏominus*—this was a guiding principle of Roman law: the (respective) owner has to bear the accidental loss. To the extent that the state is not responsible for natural disasters or the international chaos of war, it is traditionally not required to exempt the individual from the financial consequences of such a stroke of fate. Rather, it has always been part of the human condition that the individual must accept the collateral damage of historical developments. However, the randomness of the damage and its arbitrary distribution among the individuals affected contrast fundamentally with the idea of justice in the sense that all people participate equally in life's opportunities and risks.

It is therefore an old idea that the community constituted in the state operates and should operate as a mutual insurance company. Germany's Basic Law has placed the goal of realizing the welfare state on an equal footing with the principles of democracy and the rule of law. Thinking about insurance in terms of the welfare state begins with compulsory insurance for buildings against fire damage and road accident insurance and ends with social welfare measures—from classic social benefits via *Hartz IV* [German unemployment benefit enacted in 2005] to the recently introduced *Bürgergel* [German unemployment benefit introduced in 2023]. The essence of the welfare state is always also the realization of social equality. The only question is how far the state's ability to act as a pan-German insurance company can and should reach. Is the individual citizen to be guaranteed a minimum level of social subsistence or their last level of income? Should small or large companies be saved from any crisis at any price—and where does the market's tough selection process begin? Does the apartment have to be as warm as it was last winter—or should uncapped gas prices encourage people to save money? One gets the impression that the welfare state, affected by the crises of recent years—perhaps also affected by a new-found fiscal "lightness of being"—has abandoned the old model of merely providing subsistence-level aid and is replacing it with a new model of preserving existing pay and conditions. Ultimately, however, the state as a source of assistance in the face of all the vicissitudes of life goes beyond being an insurance-style instrument of risk allocation and in reality sees itself as a driver of redistribution: redistribution via taxes, from which ongoing aid is provided, or redistribution via debts, and thus across intergenerational boundaries.

However, what this type of politics cannot achieve is maintaining the efficiency of a society, of an entire economy. One external disaster such as a pandemic or a war that hits the state community as a whole must necessarily reduce the prosperity of all in this community, as economists Kai A. Konrad and Marcel Thum recently showed succinctly.[2] We can then try to mitigate the effects on individual citizens as far as possible and make distinctions according to need. But one cannot ignore the fact that the cake is getting smaller for everyone. A massive increase in prices of gas or raw materials or a slump in international demand or even a global enforcement of climate-related production and consumption restrictions cannot be ignored in the long term. The prosperity of a country can be knocked off balance, and fate takes no account of whether a society is used to enjoying vested benefits and whether a loss of prosperity is "self-inflicted" or not.

This means that if a country wants to secure prosperity for its citizens, keep its economy running, and maintain social stability, more has to be done than permanently cushioning risks and the fiction of never-ending vested benefits. Society as a whole must become more resilient. This includes not only the willingness of citizens to reduce consumption to a limited extent, but also (and even more so) the will to make a joint effort: unleashing economic power, the desire to innovate, the use of labor, observing the rules of sustainability—many things we could list here that contribute to securing Germany's prosperous future.

But this requires politicians to admit not only to the challenges of the time but also to the limits of what they can do. And it requires society, i.e., companies and citizens, not to demand that the state be a permanent guarantor of established personal prosperity.

Notes

1. Helmut Kohl in a television address, July 1, 1990.
2. Editor's note: For more from Kai A. Konrad, see his contribution "Romantic Love and Intergenerational Mobility" in the present volume, p. 103–112.

CHAPTER 10

DEMOCRATIC EQUALITY AND CHANGES IN MODERN LIBERAL DEMOCRACIES

CLAUDIA WIESNER

INTRODUCTION[1]

Representative democracy is the most well-established democratic system of government in the world. After several waves of democratization, for a couple of years it seemed to be the winner in history. A crucial principle of liberal representative democracy is that it is based on the idea of democratic equality: all individuals are considered equal and as having equal chances and rights to participate in democratic processes and institutions. But currently, representative democracy is changing, and it is under pressure. Not only are a growing number of states on a path towards illiberalism and authoritarianism, but the existing representative democracies are also challenged all over the world by democratic erosion and manifold changes. Change means, however, that there is not only erosion, but that some changes are ambivalent in their effect on representative democracy, and that, furthermore, new democratic actors and forms are also on the rise. All this, as will be argued below, affects democratic equality. However, change is inherent to democracy. Representative democracy needs to be seen in its historicity: it is constantly changing and adapting to changing societies and historical circumstances. Representative democracy in times of social media cannot imitate a Greek *polis* or a Renaissance city-state. Change is thus not per se a sign of crisis, but a characteristic of representative democracy. So, the question is from what turning point onwards change affects representative democracy so decisively that it is affected fundamentally.

Against this backdrop, this chapter has two goals. First, the state of the art of liberal representative democracy regarding the current main changes will be sketched through a short synthesis of current academic debates. It is argued that democracy is currently challenged by nine fields of change. Six of them describe changes in democracy and how it works and manifests as such, namely: democratic deconsolidation, populism, democratic backsliding, technocracy, new movements, and democratic innovations. Three other fields describe decisive changes in the societal context of democracy: the tendency towards a two-thirds society, digitalization, and the globalization trilemma. The challenges to modern liberal democracies result from an interaction between these nine problem fields. On this basis, it is discussed how these changes affect liberal democracy and to what extent they endanger the principle of democratic equality. The chapter concludes by sketching possible solutions and strategies that might strengthen democratic resilience.

A WORLDWIDE DIAGNOSIS OF DEMOCRATIC CHANGE—STATE OF THE ART

Over the last few years, crisis diagnoses for representative democracy have been abundant. Democratic theorists were the first to mark the signs of the time: J. Rancière in 1996 and later Colin Crouch spoke of "post-democracy," Peter Mair described a "hollowing out" of Western democracy, and Nadia Urbinati discussed "democracy disfigured,"[2] to name but a few. And indeed, there are several empirical indicators that underline decisive changes affecting both institutions and rights in representative democracy and its actors—citizens, politicians, civil society, parties, and government representatives. Studies mention nine fields of democratic change that are pertinent in the European Union since the beginning of the financial crisis in 2008. The first six fields describe changes in how democracy works and manifests as such:

1. Democratic deconsolidation: there are sound empirical indicators for democratic deconsolidation, as pro-democratic attitudes are currently declining at least in a number of countries. Some authors conclude that support for democracy is declining in general,[3] while others highlight that researchers must not overstate this trend.[4] However, several findings are disquieting. In the United States, less than a third of millennials believe that it is important to live in a democracy.[5] In the EU, citizen support of the EU and trust in its institutions have been declining at least temporarily during the financial crisis.[6] The debtor

countries Spain, Greece, Cyprus, Portugal, Italy, Slovenia, and Ireland have seen the largest growth in proportions of "detached" citizens. This decrease can be linked to dissatisfaction with austerity.[7]

2. Populism: populist parties and politicians have been on the rise worldwide. Election results and support for populist parties have been increasing over the last few years in most established democracies. Again, in the EU Member States since 2008 populist election results have increased decisively.[8] The electoral success of Giorgia Meloni in the EU-founding Member State of Italy in 2022 is the latest example. This rise of populism indicates a problem for representative democracy: the populist claim to incarnate the people in reality means replacing the whole of the people with a part of the people (populist supporters), excluding minorities and eliminating pluralism.[9]

3. Democratic backsliding: in some representative democratic states, right-wing populist politicians have accessed government. In most of these states, institutions and principles of representative democracy have been hollowed out. Comparative research underlines that this does

not happen immediately after election, but gradually, by governmental and political actors slowly but decisively eroding democratic principles,[10] and that democratic backsliding is enabled by permissive or even supportive attitudes among decisive parts of the population.[11] And again, the post-financial-crisis EU after 2008 has seen democratic backsliding in a number of cases. Hungary is the most prominent example, but Poland should be mentioned as well.[12] This is all the more remarkable as the EU is based on the principles of the rule of law and democracy, and hence disregarding these principles has cost the Polish and Hungarian governments repeated warnings and infringement procedures.[13]

4. Technocracy: a number of current studies claim technocracy, i.e. decisions being shifted from democratically legitimized bodies to (more) opaque expert bodies, undermines representative democracy.[14] The institutional handling of the EU's financial crisis gives strong empirical support to such criticism, as it led to huge democratic deficits, such as parliaments being bypassed, their competencies being cut down, decision-making in opaque expert circles, and an overall lack of legitimacy and

accountability of the crisis governance structures.[15] Austerity governance, in short, led to a hollowing-out of national democratic institutions and to shrinking EU support, as described above—even if one might judge it effective. This critical diagnosis holds despite the frequent statement that, in the Greek case especially, there was no alternative to austerity governance. First, there was an alternative: Greece leaving the Euro area. Second, even if this alternative is judged unattractive, austerity governance is not necessarily required to bypass representative institution. It would have been possible, for instance, to set budget limits without encroaching on national competencies or to follow the path described by national constitutions, that is, a temporary emergency regime according to constitutional rules.[16]

5. Democratic innovations:[17] a number of new tools and participatory mechanisms such as round tables or citizen budgets are aimed at enhancing partic-ipation and stakeholder involvement, and hence triggering democratic activity. Many authorities and governments, especially at local level, rely on such instruments. It is, however, questionable to what degree they indeed enhance democracy and

especially democratic equality, as mostly better educated and well-situated social groups participate. This means so far they enhance only the participation of a limited group of citizens instead of strengthening democracy overall.[18]

6. New movements: since the beginning of the EU's financial crisis we are also seeing a number of new social movements on both left and right, such as the Indignados in Spain, Pegida in Germany, or the protest movements against climate change. While this is a sign of democratic vitality on the one hand, these new movements, on the other hand, are not necessarily always supporting representative democracy. Some even act openly against it, and not only the right-wing ones.[19]

These changes in the actors and processes of representative democracy are accompanied by decisive changes in the societal context of democracy that can be summed up in three fields:

7. Two-thirds society: the tendency towards a two-thirds society is visible in a number of developed countries and, as recent studies underline, has crucial effects on democratic participation. Lower

social strata participate considerably less in elections,[20] which means that policy output to a much higher degree is legitimized by higher social strata. On the other hand, citizens from lower social strata also tend to see themselves as decoupled from the majority of the society and from representative institutions.[21] Once again, this tendency has strengthened during the EU's financial crisis. Austerity policies have hit the lower social strata in the debtor countries far more seriously, which explains why they might feel compelled to lose trust in both the EU and democracy.

8. Digitalization: understood as the process of using digitalized information or data for business interests, digitalization entails a number of challenges to core democratic principles.[22] The new currency of the digital age is no longer workforce or capital but data. Conceptions and practices of what is an individual and what an individual's inalienable democratic and human rights are have thus been hit by the effects of digitalization, that is, by digital tools, for instance by preventive police raids against innocent citizens deemed suspect by algorithms. In addition, due to digital social media, what was formerly a national public space has become split

into fragmented publics. Direct communication via the Internet comes with a promise of freedom as everyone can participate in discussions. But the Internet in general tends to reproduce and radicalize prejudicial and factional loyalties.[23] Hence Internet communication reduces social mediation and the protection of minority positions. Not only has social media frequently been shown to be a battlefield for opinion wars, it also allows populist politicians to communicate directly with their followers, as the notorious Twitter feeds of Donald Trump underline, and thus are an enabling factor if not a driver of populism.[24]

9. Globalization trilemma: formulated by Dani Rodrick,[25] the globalization trilemma states that out of three goals—namely democracy, high social standards, and unlimited free trade—nation states can achieve only two. If a state opts to participate in unrestricted free trade, this comes at the expense of either national democratic standards or social standards. The trilemma explains both the increase in technocracy and social inequality in the EU in the crisis: the EU and its Member States have largely opted for participation in both worldwide and EU-wide free trade, which has limited their

margin of maneuver for keeping up democratic and social standards in times of financial crisis.[26]

CHANGE OR CRISIS OF DEMOCRACY?

Is representative democracy just changing, or is it in crisis? In short, the answer is both. It changes, and several of the changes also challenge representative democracy. All of the fields of change concern in particular how democratic equality is realized (or not): democratic deconsolidation indicates that the belief and trust in the principles of liberal democracy, and hence in the established idea of democratic equality, are shrinking. Populism claims a version of democratic equality that only is valid for the people defined as "right" by the populists—different from liberal democratic equality, which is based on the idea that all individuals are equal and must enjoy equal rights. While the concept of the people is at the core of representative democracy, populist actors transform its meaning and (a) claim an exclusive role in representing the people, and (b) construct an essentialist and nationalist image of the people that excludes individuals deemed to be unfit. Democratic backsliding leads to the rights and rules that are the basis for enacting democratic equality being cut down. Technocracy shifts decision-making procedures from broadly legitimized decision-making bodies to expert circles—and this, again, affects democratic equality, since access to and accountability of these decision-making bodies is more opaque and more unequal than in officially legitimized bodies such as parliaments. Democratic innovations and many of the new movements both have a crucial Janus face when it comes to democratic equality: in most of the new procedures, and also in most of the new left-wing movements, participants are comparatively well educated and comparatively well situated economically. The same is not true for most right-wing movements, which tend to consist of less well educated and situated people. This means that the new procedures and movements enhance rather than decrease democratic inequality. This also goes for the challenge of a two-thirds society. Economic inequality directly affects democratic equality, as economic weakness is associated with a decoupling from democratic processes. Digitalization creates different public spaces and renders access to them more unequal than before—equal participation, or the possibility of all citizens participating equally in political life, is severely affected. Finally, the globalization trilemma describes how the capacity of states to guarantee democratic equality is limited in globalization.

Moreover, what has been said above indicates that the changes in democracy need to be looked at and studied in detail and in their interrelations. And this has several consequences for how we should see democracy. On the *theoretical and conceptual* level, representative democracy is, on one hand, structured by its institutions and laws and marked by a crucial relation between the demos, parliament, and government. Representative democracy is however not only shaped by parties, elites, and governments but also by citizens, activists, protesters, and everyday activities. Representative democracy is what its actors make of it.[27] All this lays claim to the methodological thesis that democratic change is driven by actors that *do or undo democracy.*[28] On the *ontological* level, as said in the introduction, representative democracy needs to be studied in its historicity. Change is inscribed into the nature of democracy. It is not per se a sign of crisis, but, on the contrary, it is its very condition, it is what democracy is essentially about.

Does this mean that the nine fields are just new signs of democratic change? To some extent yes, at another level no. Building on the imagery of Nadia Urbinati, it can be said that if these changes go too far, democracy is damaged, or "disfigured."[29] This happens when the defining traits, the "figure" of democracy, are no longer recognizable. Accordingly, the nine fields are not per se negative or critical for democracy. Some changes can damage democracy, and others might just change it. Technocracy, for instance, has been related to emphasizing the search for the best possible solution and effectiveness and efficiency in producing and using public goods. Seen in that way, it improves the system's output and enhances output legitimacy, and this may be regarded as beneficial for the common good. As a downside, decision-making competence has been shifting to unelected experts and administrators. Populism is based on a criticism of governing elites and an emphasis on the role of the people. This, as such, is perfectly legitimate and, moreover, the possibility of criticizing government is a defining trait of modern representative democracies and the rule of law. Digitalization and social media, finally, can be interpreted as creating new arenas and tools for democratic activity and even democratizing processes, such as in the Arab Spring. Their downside is a fragmentation of the public space and/or its usage as a battlefield for opinion wars, as well as a changing role and reduced rights of the individual citizen. The changing character of democracy therefore should be analyzed, including the Janus-faced effects of doing and undoing democracy.

DOING DEMOCRACY

In conclusion, it is crucial for liberal representative democracy that it is able to change without being disfigured. Democracy—and this is not a simple truth—depends on the people *doing democracy*. It depends on citizens, NGOs, and activists, on political parties and politicians, and indeed of these and in most cases it depends on the persons who are convinced of democracy and bear it, namely the citizens. This is why out of the processes that have been sketched above democratic deconsolidation has to be deemed the most dangerous, because it means that the very basis of democracy is crumbling. Making democracy resilient and making it work starts with the people who are convinced of democracy. Especially populist criticism of democracy is based on denouncing democracy. Importantly, such criticism cannot only be countered by downplaying it: people need to be won over for democracy in order for them to do democracy—to support it, and to become politically active.

But how can we win people over for democracy? Interestingly, academic research so far has focused more on diagnosing the crisis symptoms of democracy than on finding out what makes democracies resilient. But we can draw on findings and experiences with established democracies and successful democratic practices to draw some conclusions about what makes democracies resilient and drives people to do democracy. First, it is a standard truth in democracy research that one basis of support for a democratic system is the democracy's political output, i.e., the question of whether citizens are satisfied with the policies they have to live with. In times of economic and energy crises, this invites us to place a special focus on decreasing the effects of inflation and a lack of energy support by targeted support and redistributive politics. Second, economic inequality and social divisions challenge democratic equality and the stability of democracies, especially when societies become too fragmented or develop opposing camps. This again invites us to counteract economic inequality with redistributive policies, social services, and in particular education; and it also invites governments to aim at regulating digital public spaces and rendering access to them as equal as possible. Third, people whose experience is that their political action matters show a greater support for democracy. This is a task for authorities, but in particular for political parties, NGOs, and citizens themselves—to do democracy, and to carry as many people as possible along with them.

Notes

1. An earlier version of the following arguments has been developed in Claudia Wiesner, "Doing and Undoing Representative Democracy. Problem Diagnosis and Research Agenda" in *Democratic Crisis Revisite*: *The Dialectics of Politicisation an*•*Depoliticisation*, ed. Meike Schmidt-Gleim, Ruzha Smilova, and Claudia Wiesner (Baden-Baden: Nomos Verlagsgesellschaft mbH & Co. KG, 2022).

2. Jacques Rancière, "Demokratie und Postdemokratie" in *Politik* • *er Wahrheit*, ed. Alain Badiou, Jacques Rancière, and Rado Riha (Vienna: Turia+Kant, 1996); Colin Crouch, *Post-*•*emocracy* (Malden, MA: Polity Press, 2004); Peter Mair, *Ruling The Voi*•*: The Hollowing of Western Democracy* (London: Verso, 2013); Nadia Urbinati, *Democracy Disfigure*•*: Opinion, Truth, an*•*the People* (Cambridge, MA: Harvard University Press, 2014).

3. See for example Roberto S. Foa and Yascha Mounk, "The End of the Consolidation Paradigm: A Response to Our Critics" in *Journal of Democracy* (2017), DOI: 10.17863/ CAM.90407, Roberto S. Foa and Yascha Mounk, "The Signs of Deconsolidation," *Journal of Democracy* 28, no. 1, 2017, DOI: 10.1353/jod.2017.0000; Christopher Claasen, "In the Mood for Democracy? Democratic Support as Thermostatic Opinion" in *American Political Science Review* 114 (1), 2020, DOI: 10.1017/S0003055419000558.

4. Amy C. Alexander and Christian Welzel, "The Myth of Deconsolidation: Rising Liberalism and the Populist Reaction" in *Journal of Democracy,* 2017, https://www. journalofdemocracy.org/online-exchange-democratic-deconsolidation/ (accessed December 8, 2022); Pippa Norris, "Is Western Democracy Backsliding? Diagnosing the Risks" in *Journal of Democracy,* 2017, https://www. journalofdemocracy.org/online-exchange-democratic-deconsolidation/ (accessed December 8, 2022).

5. Yascha Mounk, *The People vs. Democracy: Why Our Freedom Is in Danger and How to Save It* (Cambridge, MA: Harvard University Press, 2018).

6. See for example Bruno Arpino and Anastassia V. Obydenkova, "Democracy and Political Trust Before and After the Great Recession 2008: The European Union and the United Nations" in *Social Indicators Research* 12 (3), 2019, DOI: 10.1007/s11205-019-02204-x; Klaus Armingeon and Kai Guthmann, "Democracy in Crisis? The Declining Support for National Democracy in European Countries, 2007–2011" in *European Journal of Political Research* 53 (3), 2014, DOI: 10.1111/1475-6765.12046.

7. Klaus Armingeon, Kai Guthmann, and David Weisstanner, "How the Euro divides the Union: The Effect of Economic Adjustment on Support for Democracy in Europe" in *Socio-Economic Review* 14 (1), 2016, DOI: 10.1093/ser/mwv028.

8. See, for example, Catherine E. De Vries, *Euroscepticism and the Future of European Integration* (Oxford: Oxford University Press, 2018); Göran Adamson, "Why Do Right-Wing Populist Parties Prosper? Twenty-One Suggestions to the Anti-Racist" in *Society* 56 (1), 2019, DOI: 10.1007/s12115-018-00323-8; Jürgen Essletzbichler, Franziska Disslbacher, and Mathias Moser, "The Victims of Neoliberal Globalisation and the Rise of the Populist Vote: a Comparative Analysis of Three Recent Electoral Decisions" in *Cambridge Journal of Regions, Economy and Society* 11 (1), DOI: 10.1093/cjres/rsx025.

9. Nadia Urbinati, *Me the People: How Populism Transforms Democracy* (Cambridge, MA: Harvard University Press, 2019); Jan-Werner Müller, *What Is Populism?* (Philadelphia: University of Pennsylvania Press Inc., 2016).

10. Steven Levitsky and Daniel Ziblatt, *How Democracies Die* (New York: Crown, 2018); Nancy Bermeo, "On Democratic Backsliding" in *Journal of Democracy* 27 (1), 2016, DOI: 10.1353/jod.2016.0012; Murat Somer,

"Understanding Turkey's Democratic Breakdown: Old vs. New and Indigenous vs. Global Authoritarianism" in *Southeast European and Black Sea Studies* 16 (4), 2016, DOI: 10.1080/14683857.2016.1246548.

11. Arlie Russell Hochschild, *Strangers in their own Land: Anger and Mourning on the American Right* (New York: The New Press, 2018); see also the classic study, Theodor W. Adorno et al., *The Authoritarian Personality* (New York: Norton, 1969).

12. Heino Nyyssönen, "The East is Different, Isn't It? – Poland and Hungary in Search of Prestige" in *Journal of Contemporary European Studies* 26 (39), 2018, DOI: 10.1080/14782804.2018.1498772.

13. European Parliament, "Rule of Law in Hungary and Poland: MEPs to take Stock of EU Actions | 04-04-2022 | News | European Parliament", https://www.europarl.europa.eu/news/en/agenda/briefing/2022-04-04/7/rule-of-law-in-hungary-and-poland-meps-to-take-stock-of-eu-actions (accessed November 11, 2022).

14. See for example Urbinati, *Democracy Disfigured*; Mounk, *The People vs. Democracy.*

15. Agustín J. Menéndez, "Hermann Heller NOW" in *European Law Journal* 21 (3), 2015, DOI: 10.1111/eulj.12135; Jonathan White, "Emergency Europe" in *Political Studies* 63 (2), 2015, DOI: 10.1111/1467-9248.12072; Aleksandra Maatsch and Ian Cooper, "Governance Without Democracy? Analysing the Role of Parliaments in European Economic Governance after the Crisis: Introduction to the Special Issue" in *Parliamentary Affairs* 70 (4), 2017, DOI: 10.1093/pa/gsx018.

16. Claudia Wiesner, "Representative Democracy in Financial Crisis Governance: New Challenges in the EU Multilevel System" in *Recalibrating Legislative-executive Relations in the European Union*, ed. Diane Fromage, Thomas Christiansen, and Anna Herranz-Sualles (Hart Publishing Ltd, 2021).

17. See for example Brigitte Geissel and Marko Joas, *Participatory Democratic Innovations in Europe: Improving the Quality of Democracy?* (Opladen: Barbara Budrich Publishers, 2013).

18. Claudia Wiesner, *Multi-Level-Governance und lokale Demokratie: Politikinnovationen im Vergleich* (Vergleichende Politikwissenschaft) (Wiesbaden: Springer VS, 2017).

19. Christian Volk, "Zwischen Entpolitisierung und Radikalisierung – Zur Theorie von Demokratie und Politik in Zeiten des Widerstands" in *Politische Vierteljahresschrift* 54 (1), 2013.

20. Armin Schäfer, Robert Vehrkamp, and Jérémie F. Gagné, "Prekäre Wahlen: Milieus und soziale Selektivität der Wahlbeteiligung bei der Bundestagswahl 2013" https://www.bertelsmann-stiftung.de/de/publikationen/publikation/did/prekaere-wahlen/ (accessed December 8, 2022).

21. Hochschild, *Strangers in their own Land*; Wiesner, *Multi-Level-Governance und lokale Demokratie.*

22. See for example Shoshana Zuboff, *The Age of Surveillance Capitalism: The Fight for the Future at the New Frontier of Power* (London: Profile Books, 2019); Evgeny Morozov, *To Save Everything, Click Here: Technology, Solutionism and the Urge to Fix Problems that Don't Exist* (London: Allen Lane, 2013).

23. Cass R. Sunstein, *Infotopia: How many Minds Produce Knowledge* (New York: Oxford University Press, 2006).

24. Terry Flew and Petros Iosifidis, "Populism, Globalisation and Social Media" in *International Communication Gazette* 225, 2019, DOI: 10.1177/1748048519880721; Andreas Jungherr, Ralph Schroeder, and Sebastian Stier, "Digital Media and the Surge of Political Outsiders: Explaining the Success of Political Challengers in the United States, Germany, and China" in *Social Media + Society* 5 (3), 2019, DOI: 10.1177/2056305119875439.

25. Dani Rodrik, *The Globalization Paradox: Democracy and the Future of the World Economy* (New York: W. W. Norton & Company, 2010).

26. Claudia Wiesner, "Free Trade versus Democracy and Social Standards in the European Union: Trade-Offs or Trilemma?" in *Politics and Governance* 7 (4), 2019, DOI: 10.17645/pag.v7i4.2272.

27. Claudia Wiesner, "Politicisation, Politics and Democracy" in *Rethinking Politicisation in Politics, Sociology and International Relations*, ed. Claudia Wiesner (Cham: Springer International Publishing, 2021).

28. Wiesner, "Doing and Undoing Representative Democracy."

29. Urbinati, *Democracy Disfigured*.

CHAPTER 11

THE WORLD AFTER EMPIRE: ON THE ROLE OF TRADE IN EFFORTS AT MAKING THE WORLD MORE EQUAL

MATHIAS RISSE

INTRODUCTION: HOW TRADE HAS MADE THE WORLD

What I would like to cover here is a set of considerations from philosophy, history, and political science that highlight the importance of trade in creating a more equal world. Let me begin with a historical perspective on how incredibly important trade has always been for making the world that we inhabit.

Humanity has come out of an evolutionary context of small groups of humans—and in order to get beyond what these small-group contexts make possible, our ancestors had to engage in exchanges with others. People are good at producing certain things, and the things we are not good at producing ourselves we can get by exchange, which then vastly increases the range of things to which we have access. Trade has always been an activity that channels both cooperative and competitive behavior in human beings. By doing so, trade has not just shaped the social and political structures of the world but has also shaped how the land itself in different regions of the world has been used. What we are doing with territory is shaped by trade—and, therefore, so is what people can do who live there, and how the demographics of the regions in question unfold.

Sugar is a great example to illustrate this. Sugar was cultivated first in New Guinea, spread across Asia, and was then taken up by Muslim traders. Muslim traders brought sugar to Europe, where it became indispensable for many kinds of enjoyment. In fact, it became so important for Europeans that whole swaths of land, islands in the Caribbean as well as parts of South and Central America, were used for sugar plantations to satisfy that need. Millions of Africans were kidnapped to do the backbreaking labor required to make sugar plantations profitable after Europeans had driven the indigenous people in these parts of the Americas to extinction. The point is that not just things, practices, ideas, and products get exchanged in trade relations, but that the movement of people and what we do with territory is also determined by trade.

Another example is coffee. Originally from Ethiopia, coffee quickly assumed the functions we know today: both as a social lubricant and as a stimulant making the often monotonous and otherwise fatiguing flow of days easier. Again, the Muslim world got there first before coffee traveled to Europe, starting in Vienna. Coffee houses played an enormous role in Europe's social life in the 17th and 18th centuries. It is hard to understand the Enlightenment as an intellectual and political movement without the coffee houses that provided the locations for the public sphere of those days. One purpose of European colonialism was to see where Europeans could get the things they liked—and coffee was high on that list. Europeans told certain regions of the world, such as Indonesia and parts of the Americas, that their role in the colonial structures was to produce coffee and brutalized these regions into compliance. Again, population movements followed, and what people could do in those regions was subsequently limited by these colonial prescriptions that were driven by trade-related ambitions. Sugar and coffee are both commodities based on plants, but there are many more (and quite varied) examples to illustrate how our world has always been shaped by trade. Trade really has made the world.

THE COMPARATIVE ADVANTAGE ARGUMENT

How do economists and philosophers respectively think about trade? In the early 19th century, economist David Ricardo formulated a brilliant argument that set the stage for much subsequent intellectual work and became politically enormously influential. The argument is simple but not even Adam Smith—the founding spirit of contemporary economics—had fully come to it. It took Ricardo to formulate the standard economic argument for free trade, whose central theme is comparative advantage. One can think of comparative advantage in two different ways: it could be a way of thinking about how good I am at doing something compared to how good someone else (or another country) is at it; or else it could be a term encapsulating the notion that I am better at certain things than I am at doing other things. The more interesting sense of comparative advantage in the trade context is the latter; and then the point is that I as a trading entity, as a person or a country, should think about what I am best at compared to other things that I could do. What is the best use of my time? There are simplifying assumptions here, but the idea is that if I have one hour, what kind of thing can I produce most of? Once I know, I do only that. I specialize in the production of what I am best at (my comparative advantage), and then everything else I would like to possess I can obtain by exchanging it for what I am best at producing on my own terms.

To appreciate the power of this argument, take Bill Gates for example. Gates is very good at developing software. But suppose he is actually better than any of us at everything. The fact that Gates is best at everything does not matter for his comparative advantage. As long as he is best on his own terms at producing software, he should still spend all his time on software and get everything else by exchanging software for it. The argument works unilaterally. That is, even if you do not like to trade with me, these considerations drawing on comparative advantage provide me with an argument as to why I should try to trade with you. Only because you are irrationally focused on doing too many things yourself does not mean I should do the same.

Sometimes economists say this comparative advantage argument is a purely self-interested argument and has nothing to do with ethics or fairness. That is, it is an argument that appeals to any given country's rationality, and no other considerations need enter to make trade an appealing course of action. And the way I have stated this argument so far, that is true. But the comparative advantage argument is not ultimately compelling unless you also bring in fairness considerations (and this is where the philosophers enter). Consider first the international domain. Let us say I want to send out my ships to trade. If the seas are not safe for my ships, if there's no international safety and security structure, I can be persuaded by the comparative advantage argument all I like, but I am not going to get to trade. Say, if all ships off the coast of Somalia get kidnapped, trade is impossible in that region. Therefore, we need an international cooperative system to maintain trade. That means trade—even though it is unilaterally rational—is not actually unilaterally possible. Instead, trade is something we can only do together. And if that is the case, we need to think about what an internationally fair distribution of the gains from trade looks like. This is the international aspect of fairness.

Fairness also matters domestically. The comparative advantage argument suggests that every country should go through a self-exploratory process to find out what they are best at. But once you are specializing on a certain good, you are disadvantaging all sorts of other things that are also happening in your country. Other people in your country—fellow citizens—need to be taken care of as well because they are part of the same structure for which we need to make policy. We therefore need to have a balanced trade policy with certain transfers domestically, to aid people who would otherwise lose out. This is the second reason we have to design trade fairly in ways that make sense for everybody. Trade really is good, and although in real life the argument looks much more complicated, it does hold up well. But we must never stop thinking about how we are implementing trade in an international and domestic system so that internationally countries are treated in some way approximating a status as equal participants in an international trade regime, and domestically individual citizens are treated as equal citizens.

A HISTORICAL PERSPECTIVE: DESIGNING A
TRADE REGIME AFTER EMPIRE

World War II put an end to centuries of empires. Empires were exhausted and a great number of resistance movements had been inspired by activities during the war. As empires were coming to an end, a new global political and economic system was needed. The United Nations emerges at the end of the war to pioneer novel ways of coordinating political and economic systems on a global scale. Various ways of integrating the newly decolonized countries—of which there were dozens and dozens—as something approximating equal players in a world system were explored within the United Nations context. However, this process of emancipation set in motion after World War II was a long road to disappointment for many of the new countries. It was a long road of failed integration, and roughly speaking, that's where we still are. Failures in the domain of trade stand out.

Following the enormous administrative reforms that President Franklin Delano Roosevelt had set in motion in the United States in the 1930s, the United Nations basically became a global projection of the American New Deal. The New Deal captured a new level of sophistication in the domain of public administration in ways that also sought to integrate considerations of social justice—in ways that had just not been possible previously because the necessary logistical and administrative capacities had not been available. But once thinking about public administration had changed dramatically in the domestic context, it was tempting and sensible to attempt something of that sort on the much larger scale of the world as a whole. As a result, the United Nations as well as various closely connected organizations like the World Bank and the International Monetary Fund were created. In addition, there was supposed to be such an organization specifically for trade, an organization called the International Trade Organization (ITO). The ITO was mapped out in Havana at one of the biggest international conferences that had ever happened. The conference was meant to create a commercial space for the countries that at this stage people already knew would be decolonized. The idea was to make them not just part of the UN, but to create a commercial space where they could operate as something approximating equal players in a world of nation states.

But the ITO never materialized because in the end the US vetoed the plans. Instead, we got the General Agreement on Tariffs and Trade (GATT), which was basically a trade arrangement among wealthy countries only. Roughly speaking, the wealthy countries did not have enough political motivation to create a commercial space for everyone. Therefore, they created a commercial space limited to a small club of countries. But the UN is an absolutely fascinating organization and was especially so in the 1950s and into the 1960s. It took on a life of its own beyond what its American creators had anticipated (and bargained for). The UN bureaucracy became a hotbed of intellectuals from around the world engaged in forward-looking thinking. For example, Swedish economist Gunnar Myrdal argued that if we have something resembling a globally projected New Deal, we should turn the UN into a global welfare state. The idea did not go anywhere and today it would be laughed at. But at the time, it was at least a serious suggestion from someone who was later awarded one of the first Nobel Prizes in Economics.

The most important radical intellectual at the UN at this period was Argentine economist Raúl Prebisch, often called the "Keynes of the South." Prebisch was the central thinker on how to integrate the newly decolonized countries into this new world, replacing the dying world of empires. Two big things happened in the 1960s and the 1970s under Prebisch's influence. First of all, he founded the UN Conference on

Trade and Development (UNCTAD), a place for the newly decolonized countries to congregate and to start formulating their interests. It was the first time most of the countries that were not previously colonizers got organized together. And then something truly remarkable happened—the oil shock of the 1970s. The oil-exporting countries showed the rest of the world that without oil things looked bleak. They proved that commodity producers had power. The other UNCTAD members realized that if this can be done with one commodity, it can be done writ large by finding weak spots where they are needed in the global economy. The result was the New International Economic Order (NIEO) in the 1970s, the most powerful alliance of developing countries (the nomenclature at the time) ever assembled. These countries got very close to changing the world in dramatic ways. But it speaks to itself that there's almost no collective memory of that at all. It all went away. Let us take a closer look at what happened.

The developing nations of UNCTAD put together a list of demands laying out what needed to happen to create a world of equal countries in the commercial spaces as was supposed to be designed under the aegis of the ITO. These nations were so powerful at the time that they managed to pass their proposals at the UN. The wealthy countries did not see much of a choice and agreed. A key demand of the NIEO was technology transfer. The developing countries did not just want to produce commodities. They wanted their own industrialization, and for that to happen, they needed patent sharing. Technology transfer was meant to make up for the colonial system which was in force when the industrial revolution took place. Not only was there no technology transfer during colonial times, but all fledgling operations that happened in the colonies were taken away. Industrialization was practically prohibited in the colonies. Technological transfer was therefore a central element in creating a world with a shared commercial space.

What then happened to these initiatives? Henry Kissinger. One of the many things that Henry Kissinger did was to dissolve the NIEO alliance with devastating effect on the mobilizing potential of developing countries. Kissinger employed a divide-and-conquer strategy, which succeeded because developing countries did not have very much in common. They were very different places all around the world. If all you have in common is that you are considered "developing" in a dichotomy between developed and developing, your alliance can easily be broken apart by a shrewd player like Kissinger. By the end of the 1970s the alliance just evaporated. That is also why most people today have never heard of the NIEO.

One last-ditch effort was made. Former German Chancellor Willy Brandt was called in by the UN, as he was known to be somebody who could bring parties together. He had done so for East and West, so the UN thought that if anybody can bring together North and South, which was the nomenclature at that time, then it was Willy Brandt. As a result, Brandt wrote a still highly readable report, titled "North-South: Program for Survival." But this report too just went away, more or less dead off the press.

At this point neoliberalism, driven by economists such as Friedrich August von Hayek and Milton Friedman, took hold. Gunnar Myrdal was awarded the Nobel Prize in Economics the same year as Hayek. And not only did Myrdal refuse to accept the prize, but he also advocated for the abolition of the prize if it were awarded to people like Hayek. That is how strong the animosity towards neoliberalism was in certain circles. But neoliberalism took over the world, with its emphasis on market action rather than the kind of state intervention domestically and internationally that had been the dominant paradigm in the postwar period until then. This led to a kind of amnesia about all the fascinating things (especially the emancipatory efforts around developing countries) that had happened before. The 1980s are generally known as a dead decade from the standpoint of development (as basically nothing happened), and typically what people know about development policy and organization starts with the 1990s.

In the 1990s we finally get a global trade organization; but it is not the ITO, rather the World Trade Organization (WTO). The WTO is only a faint shadow of what was intended with the ITO in the 1940s. In particular, all plans for technology transfer were rejected. Instead, we got TRIPS (the Agreement on Trade-Related Aspects of Intellectual Property Rights), which makes technology transfer a lot harder through the implementation of massive patent protection that the developing countries had to accept in order to get some access to global markets. Developing countries conceded a lot of things *ex ante* and did not get much in return.

TRUMP, COVID, AND THE STATE OF TECHNOLOGY TRANSFER

The situation was bad enough when Donald Trump came to power in the United States, immediately starting a new style of trade policy. His policy was not entirely idiosyncratic, though: it is a radical and bluntly undiplomatic version of what has been happening all over the world. International agreements are replaced with insistence on autarky, on becoming independent in different regards. Unilateral or at most plurilateral trade arrangements are pursued, rather than global arrangements. One particular day, new Trump measures came in that so extravagantly violated the letter and spirit of WTO arrangements that the press proclaimed the death of the WTO. The effects of these measures are still with us. A policy that Obama started but which Trump continued on a larger scale was to not approve judges for the WTO's Appellate Body. The Appellate Court was one really good thing about the WTO because its decisions had "teeth." But this only works if countries abide by it by and large—and if there is an Appellate Court at all. The US just stopped approving judges for the court. We now see a general trend in many countries' trade policy to go it alone. Recent developments surrounding the WTO have been somewhat better. But if one president withdraws American participation, the next one (Joe Biden) will not simply restore everything to where it was. International agreements typically come with concessions that involve a decrease in control that states

have over certain domains—and they would put themselves in a situation like that only under particular
circumstances.

The COVID-19 pandemic was a global stress test.
Things looked promising for a while and there was a
lot of talk about global sharing of vaccines. Everybody
was excited, but it all fell apart. The World Health
Organization (WHO) and the WTO were all involved,
particularly the WHO. COVID would have been a great
opportunity for global solidarity. But despite all the
promises, there was in the end much more pretense than
reality. BioNTech, for example, is producing vaccines
in Africa—which of course is great. But what it means
is that they are putting containers there and send their
own people; they are not sharing anything that would
empower actors in Africa to catch up on the production
of technologically sophisticated products. So, despite all
the promising rhetoric, we are not actually doing any
technology transfer. As a global stress test, COVID was
a failure. South Africa, for example, was especially badly
hit by COVID and needed vaccinations. But vaccination
rates in Africa are substantially below what they are in
many other places.

Technology transfer can still happen. And it badly
needs to happen. But this is something that we need
to advocate for, as citizens. The fact that people today

do not know about the New International Economic Order says a lot about how people think about these policy spaces.

WHERE DO THINGS STAND?

Our international organizations are not in good shape. The global financial system no longer benefits the wealthy as much as it used to, but by and large, we still have a system in which capital can move with ease. Globalization still works for the wealthy. Astronomical amounts of money are held in offshore tax havens beyond the reach of public taxation. Opacity is the norm in the financial system. There's a litany of challenges for which we need global cooperation. We need to put our heads together to address things like climate change and the arrival of AI. The international organizations that are now ailing are not creating a world where countries operate as something approximating equals. That is a real problem right now. Trade, of course, is still good and important, and it continues to bring people together, even if often not quite at the global level. Trade continues to create wealth. But we find that if that wealth is not distributed fairly, political reactions undermine the potential of trade.

All this is part of a long history of wealthy countries failing to take the rest of the world seriously. We should therefore not be surprised if much of the rest of the world does not answer our call when Europe is in trouble with the Russians attacking Ukraine. These nations will say, "Well, what have you ever done for us? There are so many conflicts like that in other parts of the world, and you did not care one bit. Do not now count on our help or solidarity."

Sometimes I think controversial German thinker Carl Schmitt was right. Schmitt argued that the colonial empires would eventually be replaced by what he called "great spaces," basically countries with security zones around them. Today we see the Russians, the Chinese, and also the Americans insisting on such security zones. So, we do see some trends in that direction, but overall, this may or may not be the trend in the long term. It is much too early to tell. To my mind, the most important thing to say about the current state of the economic order is that we still have a version of globalization. It is, however, what one might call a plutocratically highly constrained globalization. The wealthiest still benefit. If one is properly connected, finances can easily be moved to tax havens. We also find that developed countries are faced with populism because redistribution does not happen properly. There is no sophisticated industrial policy, certainly not in the US, that could make sure people broadly benefit from trade and from globalization. Developing countries, on the other hand, are suffering from extremely constrained policy spaces because the international commercial space was never created in a way that made sense for them in any way. We have a long way to go in the creation of a trade system that advances global equality. But we must not abandon this goal.

CHAPTER 12

A NEW ERA OF TRADE POLICY AND POWER POLITICS

GABRIEL FELBERMAYR

INTRODUCTION

With the war in Ukraine, power politics is back after having seemed an ancient relic for a historically brief period between 1990 and 2010.[1] There are many reasons for its return. One is economic inequality, which has risen sharply over the past two decades, despite respectable economic growth. In many countries, this has led to polarization in domestic politics, accompanied by aggressive zero-sum rhetoric in foreign policy.

Ever since states have competed for power and political influence, they have used economic as well as military means. History is full of examples of this. Compared to earlier centuries, however, the modern world is much more interconnected economically.

In their book *War by Other Means* (2016), Robert Blackwill and Jennifer Harris have described how modern economic wars can be organized and won.[2] Daniel Drezner, Henry Farrell, and Abraham Newman (2021) describe in detail how states can use their economic interdependence in value networks to geostrategic ends.[3] These are just some examples of a body of literature that has been growing rapidly in recent years and especially months. Against the background of changed conditions, foreign trade policy must be fundamentally rethought. In this essay, we will discuss primarily the use of trade policy instruments for geopolitical purposes—geoeconomics.

THE SECURITY EXTERNALITY

Adam Smith's *Wealth of Nations* of 1776 gives us a good indication of how old thinking about geoeconomics is. Famously, the author convincingly celebrates the division of labor on the one hand. Nevertheless, he is aware that the division of labor also creates dependencies that can be exploited opportunistically. He illustrates this using the example of the competition between England and Holland, and writes "... defence, however, is of much more importance than opulence."[4] Thus, for security reasons, it may be necessary to restrict foreign trade. Smith therefore considers the Navigation Acts that deny Dutch ships access to English ports, to be "...perhaps the wisest of all commercial regulations of England."[5]

The legitimacy of trade restrictions for reasons of security is also laid down in the General Agreement on Tariffs and Trade (GATT, 1948), in which Article XXI allows exceptions for national security. This provision has been used in recent years, having been taboo for a long time. However, the system of world trade has inherent difficulties with national security issues, as it has been designed to achieve reciprocal increases in prosperity in a context of positive-sum games. It cannot deal with the zero-sum logic of international rivalries; the permitted sanction options are too weak for this.

State interventions in free trade can be justified in terms of welfare economics, even if they have economic costs. After all, when companies make decisions about where they source their raw materials or merchandise from and where they deliver to, they regularly ignore the fact that their actions may have foreign policy implications. This is usually completely rational, because even large companies are too small for their microeconomic activities to change the balance of power. However, the sum of all decisions may give rise to outcomes that are detrimental to the common good, because they result, for example, in an excessive concentration on a few suppliers or supplier countries. This means that a country runs the risk of being politically blackmailed by a trading partner who exploits its economic dependencies opportunistically. This is what we might call a security externality.

In addition, companies can often rationally expect the state to help when deliveries from abroad no longer arrive. As a result, they are always tempted to take too many risks and focus their sourcing and sales strategies on too few countries if this saves money. This is a case of moral hazard, the reduction of which may also require government intervention.

The question now is which instruments are available and which should be used. This is currently the subject of heated debate. It is clear that a range of foreign trade policy instruments already exists. However, these are often not very well targeted. In addition, there is always the danger that foreign trade protectionism will be misused for the purpose of clientelism.

DANGEROUS DEPENDENCIES EVERYWHERE?

It is surprisingly difficult to accurately identify dangerous dependencies, as there is usually a lack of necessary data. Nevertheless, we can still make some observations. On the one hand, it is crucial to take account of *all* economic interdependencies and not just goods such as steel, aluminum, batteries, chips, and pharmaceutical products. Heavy dependencies can also exist in the case of various services, from computer operating systems and mobile phones to financial services. In addition, we should look not just at international trade but also at the activities of foreign companies at home and domestic companies abroad. And finally, dependencies can also be found in the intangible property sector, such as in the exploitation of foreign patents.

Germany is a member of the highly integrated EU Single Market and part of the EU Customs Union. It has no independent trade policy. Therefore, we should analyze dependencies at EU level not at national level.

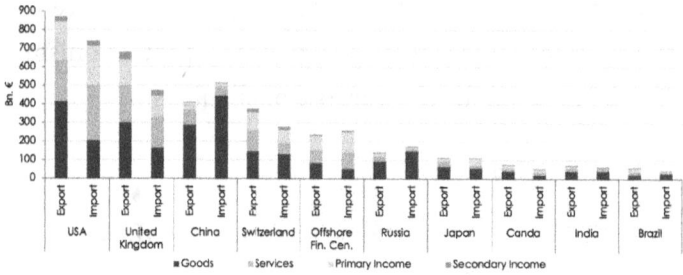

Fig. 1: *EU27 balance of payments with the most important partner countries, 2021*

Source: Eurostat; author's diagram

If we are looking for the strategically most important economic partners, we should examine not only trade in goods but the entire balance of payments. Fig. 1 shows that in the case of the EU27, the USA remains the most important economic partner, followed by the United Kingdom. China only comes in third place, followed relatively closely by Switzerland, which is 160 times smaller in terms of population size. If we are looking just at trade in goods, then China dominates. However, in the area of trade in services and primary income (income from foreign investments), China is only of minor importance. Trade with both the US and the UK is dominated by services in terms of imports; services also predominate in trade with offshore financial centers, which in economic terms are often associated with English-speaking countries. On the export side, goods are more important for all the EU's trading partners, but in many countries revenues from service exports and foreign investments exceed revenues from the export of goods. It is therefore inappropriate to focus one-sidedly on the trade in goods.

What this more comprehensive view of the balance of payments also makes clear is that the EU's trade relations are far more balanced than is often assumed. This is extremely pertinent from a geoeconomic perspective. If the EU risks being obstructed by US trade policy when exporting goods, for example, it can counteract this when it comes to importing services.

In order to be able to draw conclusions at the level of goods, it is interesting to take a look at the detailed trade statistics. In 2019 customs statistics record that the EU imported from outside the customs area a total of 10,280 different types of goods worth 1,935 billion Euros. Of these products 227 came from a single country; in 193 of these cases the import value was less than 50,000 Euros. The goods include lots of specialty foods that, by definition, can only come from a single country, such as tequila from Mexico or Gruyère from Switzerland.

The trade statistics show 779 products with an import value of 3.5 billion Euros came from a maximum of three different supplier countries, which is 0.2 percent of the total import value. The statistics therefore do not reveal a high level of dependence on individual importing countries. Nevertheless, important industrial raw materials such as lead, thallium, barium, beryllium, lithium, and platinum belong in this group. In 2019 uranium ore (with an import value of 74 million Euros) came from just two supplier countries, including Russia. Specialist substances crucial to the pharmaceutical industry such as chloroethylene, anthraquinone, and fenproporex are also in this group. And finally, there are highly specialized goods, such as telecommunications satellites, refrigeration vessels, and dredgers, which the EU only procures from a maximum of three countries.

However, trade data alone are not sufficient in assessing dependencies. For a reliable analysis, it would be necessary to know the production volumes of the individual countries at product level. Here the data situation is significantly worse than in the case of trade statistics. In addition, we would have to know what added value is associated with the use of goods and export. This would require input/output data at company level. However, the OECD's current harmonized input/output tables only contain information on 45 broadly defined sectors. Even with more detailed data, it is difficult to draw reliable conclusions about which imported goods or services are really essential, because the substitutability of imports with alternatives can only be roughly estimated and appears much more difficult in the short term than in the long term. So it follows that a clear identification of strategic goods on the basis of objective data is almost impossible.

PROTECTIONIST MEASURES ARE BECOMING MORE FREQUENT AND ARE EXPENSIVE

Over the last 15 years, the number of import restrictions has grown steadily in both the goods and services trade (see Fig. 2). The *Global Trade Alert* project at the University of St. Gallen calculates a net figure of around 18,000 restrictive measures in the goods trade alone at the end of 2022.[6] This calculation does not make a distinction between whether these measures demonstrating a classic "beggar-thy-neighbor" motivation[7] were introduced for redistribution reasons or whether they are geoeconomically motivated. In any case, the number of new restrictive measures reached a peak of almost 3,000 in 2020; since then it has been falling again. The number of export subsidies is significantly fewer, with a net figure of around 5,000 measures, but this too is growing steadily.

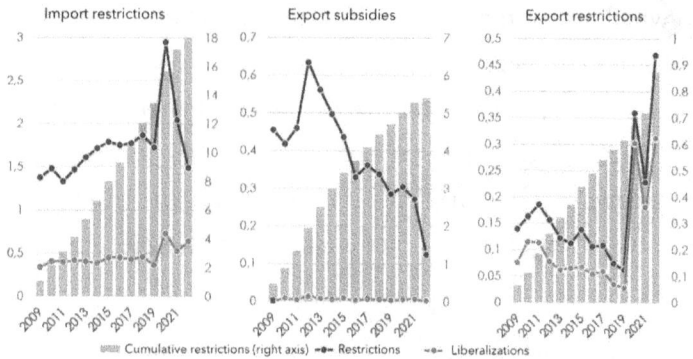

Fig. 2: *Number of trade-policy measures worldwide in thousands, 2008–22*

Source: Global Trade Alert, author's calculation and diagram. Left axis: number of new measures per year; right axis: net figure.

Since 2020 there has been a real boom in export restrictions; the net figure is now around 1,000, while in 2019 it was still around 600. In this context it is noticeable that the measures are short-lived and are often quickly lifted again. Export restrictions are particularly problematic because they create artificial shortages in the importing countries. In recent years, they have been widely used in the health and food sectors to keep down domestic prices of critical goods. This tactic is believed to be a major reason why concerns about the availability of critical goods have increased globally, as deliveries from abroad are perceived as increasingly precarious. From an economic perspective, however, these restrictions are extremely harmful: in the face of global supply shocks, they destroy the insurance role of foreign trade and reduce the welfare effect of integrated markets.[8]

Since around 2008, increasing protectionism has led to a slowdown in the growth of international trade, although other determinants are also important, such as the normalization of China's economic model away from a drastic over-specialization in tradable goods, or the phasing out of special features provided for by the creation of the WTO. Before that, for about 20 years, the trade in goods grew much faster than the production of goods. Since then, both factors have been growing at about the same rate despite significant fluctuations—most recently due to the COVID-19 crisis. With this, the phase of *hyperglobalization*[9] has indeed come to an end and the phase of *slowbalization*[10] has begun. Despite all these risks, deglobalization—a long-term decline in world trade—is somewhat unlikely.[11]

Trade restrictions, regardless of their motivation, are generally expensive from an economic point of view. In a recent study,[12] Peter Eppinger et al. show that a permanent interruption in the total trade of countries would be associated with long-term losses in purchasing power of between 6 percent (USA) and 80 percent (Luxembourg) compared to the base year (2014). In other countries, the study showed that the loss would be, depending on the size and degree of openness of the economy in question, around 20 percent in Germany, 27 percent in Austria, and 38 percent in the Netherlands. If trade in raw materials and intermediate products along the supply chain alone were interrupted, the losses would be around half as great on average. If the EU Single Market were to remain in operation, the losses for the EU states would roughly be halved again. The cash value of the loss of income can quickly amount to several tens of thousands of Euros per person, or—based on a family— the value of a mid-range car.

During the COVID-19 crisis, it was repeatedly argued that foreign trade created vulnerability. Indeed, a loss of production abroad—for example due to massive quarantine measures such as in China in spring 2020—also leads to production losses in the EU and Germany via the global value chains, because a lack of raw materials and intermediate products arises. This was clearly felt in Europe over several months. If countries were not dependent on imported raw materials and intermediate products, these negative effects would disappear. However, the international division of labor along supply chains brings welfare gains that would then have to be foregone. Using the COVID-19 restrictions in China, Eppinger et al. show that the advantage of less vulnerability due to local production stoppages would be smaller by about one whole order of magnitude than the welfare loss brought about by the complete abandonment of the international division of labor.[13]

Protectionist measures can have different motivations. Alongside goals of redistributive policy, the classic constructive goal of tapping welfare potential through the international division of labor, or the destructive goal of manipulating the terms of trade in favor of one's own country, other non-trade policy goals have come to the fore in recent years. These are very diverse and are pursued using a variety of instruments. First of all, they can be found in the trade agreements of advanced economies such as the EU. Through its trade agreements, the EU offers partner countries improved market access in Europe, but in return requires compliance with standards that go beyond classic trade policy, which countries would often be unwilling to meet without the incentives coming from Europe.

NEGATIVE SANCTIONS IN TRADE LAW
AND IN THE GEOECONOMY

But classic (negative) sanctions that deny market access to foreign importers and exporters have also been used more frequently in recent years. In 2022 the Global Sanctions Database reveals the existence of almost 600 active sanctions regimes. These are bilateral relations between countries between which official economic sanctions are active that are not primarily motivated by trade policy.[14] Such measures do not fall within the real scope of the WTO but are typically (implicitly) covered by Art. XXI of GATT.

The database lists the stated primary political goal of the sanctions in each case. It turns out that the goals are diverse. They range from a change in policy in the target country to destabilizing a regime to resolving a territorial conflict, from preventing war and fighting terrorism to ending a war, restoring human rights, and re-establishing democracy.

In addition to geoeconomic sanctions, sanctions play an important and constructive role in the "normal" foreign trade regulations of the WTO. They are necessary for the stability of an open trading system because countries focused on self-interest have strong incentives to deviate from free trade if they can do so without consequences. From the point of view of an individual country, free trade is not optimal—this has been proven by the so-called optimal tariff theory at least since the 1950s.[15] This is because a wisely chosen import tariff (or an export tax) can improve the conditions of exchange, including the idea of attracting foreign companies by means of subsidies for local production instead of exports, and even the use of trade policy measures for redistributive reasons.

The problem with this policy is that it cannot be generalized. If all countries act in this way, then the trading partners are in general collectively worse off. Moreover, they cannot escape this "prisoner's dilemma" because the best response to a foreign import tariff is another import tariff. The WTO offers a way out: it provides a forum for repeated interactions between countries and a protocol for sanctioning violations of the rules. Countries harmed by an illegitimate import tariff (or other measure) enacted by a trading partner may impose an equivalent measure that negates the hoped-for advantage of the rule-breaking country. With the prospect of this reaction, the incentives for setting an optimal tariff disappear.

So it is the threat of tariffs that makes a liberal trade regime possible in the first place. In the ideal case, the imposition of the sanction is not necessary at all, because unlawful behavior does not even occur. In the context of GATT and the WTO, this has worked very well for many decades. The permissible sanctions in commercial law are nevertheless calibrated in such a way that they trigger compensation for damage in the economic sense. However, if the violation of the rules is not at all about economic advantages but about power politics, then the threatened WTO sanction is not powerful enough.

Regardless of how sanctions are justified, they always have one thing in common: their real impact is deployed, if they have one at all, during the threat phase and not when they are imposed. The threat of a negative sanction or even the promise of a positive sanction can, if the advertised measure is calibrated appropriately, change the behavior of the target country because its cost-benefit calculation changes. For example, due to an advertised sanction a breach of the rules could not achieve any positive net benefit for a government and is therefore not done. So negative sanctions do not have to be used at all. However, if the rules are broken anyway, for example because the threat of sanctions was considered too weak, then the sanctions must be imposed—otherwise the threatening country loses all credibility—but a quick impact is highly unlikely, since the country is breaking the rules precisely because the net benefit remains positive despite the implemented threat of sanctions. This means that the empirical observation of successful sanctions in about 40 percent of all instances of sanctions and often only after many years is not at all surprising. The promise of positive sanctions, on the other hand, must be kept if it is successful, because otherwise the country loses credibility and the next promise has no impact.

In order to perfect sanctions as a geoeconomic tool, a government must obtain sufficiently good and complete information about their competitor; only then can it know how to design its threats of sanctions correctly. If such threats are too powerful, they are not very credible, because every sanction also has an economic impact on the sanctioning country. If they are calibrated too weakly, they do not work. Since the net benefit of rule-breaking by a geoeconomic competitor is to be assessed not only in economic terms, the government must also know their competitor's political preferences, costs, benefits, and options in addition to the expected economic impacts at home and abroad.

The government should also create a good structure for a sanctions process. In the end, it must be possible to impose threatened sanctions even if they entail high costs domestically. Therefore, transparent decision-making processes are required. In addition, speed is of the essence when imposing sanctions—if discussions take months, the impact will fizzle out. The EU Commission's planned Anti-coercion Instrument was intended to improve this very procedure because it accelerates the process and makes threats of sanctions more credible.

Above all, however, one thing is crucial for both positive and negative sanctions: the size and depth of the market, access to which could be restricted by sanctions. For the EU, this is the Single Market. Brexit has made it smaller, thus reducing the EU's ability to impose sanctions. The Single Market has also not undergone further expansion in recent years; this makes sanctions less painful for trading partners. And finally, the low level of economic growth in the EU is also a stumbling block.

CONCLUSIONS

Geopolitical conflicts are increasingly being staged using economic means. This is why Blackwill and Harris speak of "war by other means."[16] The West's sanctions against Russia after the attack on Ukraine and Russia's counter-sanctions are examples of the use of economic interdependence as a weapon.

It has been clear since at least February 2022 that the phase of geopolitical calm in the global economy is likely to be over for good. The new era that was often discussed in politics in 2022 actually emerged around the year 2008. Since then, the world trade in goods has not grown faster than global goods production. The number of protectionist measures is increasing. While around 200 economic sanctions were still active at country-to-country level 15 years ago, in 2022 the number has risen to some 600. The use of negative economic sanctions for geopolitical purposes may be more humane than the use of arms; nevertheless, it is expensive and has side effects. It is therefore very important that governments are well informed about their geostrategic rivals, that they are well aware of their own vulnerabilities, and that they modernize the geoeconomic toolkit. They need to increase their knowledge of global supply chains and better understand corporate incentives so that they can act rationally.

Clearly the state can successfully justify interventions in free trade in light of geopolitical tensions, because companies do not internalize the power-political effects of their import or export decisions—even large corporations are systemically too insignificant for this. It is therefore a question of minimizing a security externality.

Protectionism is not a suitable means of combating inequality, however. Much more effective and efficient instruments are available for this purpose. Yet such instruments must actually be implemented so that the advantages of the international division of labor reach as many people as possible. If this does not happen, then there is a risk that redistributive goals will influence the shaping of foreign policy, thereby narrowing the scope for cooperative solutions.

However, when it comes to the security externality, everything that helps companies to diversify their procurement and sales markets is useful. High tariffs are certainly not conducive to this; on the contrary, trade agreements such as that between the EU and Korea create opportunities for diversification under conditions of legal certainty. The German federal government's credit guarantees, which have so far only been available for export transactions, should also be available for use in imports. Overall, politicians should ensure the consistency of their overall approach. If procurement diversification is to increase in order to reduce the security externality, a supply-chain law that incurs additional fixed costs for each supplier used could turn out to have a boomerang effect. Likewise, generous aid to companies with supply-chain problems could be detrimental in the long run, because this consolidates the expectation that, in the case of geoeconomically caused supply crises, state aid will compensate for a prior narrowing of the supplier base. Such "fully comprehensive insurance" for companies in the event of production failures leads to excessive risk-taking and increases the security externality.

But diversification does not always help, because in the case of many raw materials there is only a very limited number of supplier countries. It can therefore make sense for the EU countries to set up joint strategic reserves for important raw materials and then use them jointly. In addition, tax incentives for warehousing and for promoting recycling (urban mining, circular economy) could represent efficient and effective instruments for increasing companies' resilience and thus reducing the vulnerability of governments to blackmail. A new kind of foreign trade diplomacy and strategic partnerships to pursue a *European interest* should also be at the very top of the list of priorities.

Geoeconomically, the EU's most important resource is the Single Market. The EU and the Member States should always bear this in mind when developing the new foreign trade strategy, Open Strategic Autonomy. The deeper, more innovative, larger, and more dynamic its own market is, the more the EU can make an impression on non-member countries by threatening to refuse market access. Only then will new instruments such as the Carbon Border Adjustment Mechanism, the Anti-coercion Instrument, or the International Procurement Instrument be truly effective.

Notes

1. Francis Fukuyama, *The En∢ of History an∢ the Last Man* (New York: Penguin, 2012).

2. Robert D. Blackwill and Jennifer M. Harris, *War by Other Means: Geoeconomics an∢ Statecraft* (Cambridge, MA: Harvard University Press, 2016).

3. Daniel Drezner, Henry Farrell, and Abraham Newman, *The Uses an∢ Abuses of Weaponize∢ Inter∢epen∢ence* (Washington: Brookings Institution Press, 2021).

4. Adam Smith, *An Inquiry into the Nature an∢ Causes of the Wealth of Nations* [1776] (Chicago: University of Chicago Press, 1977), vol. IV, chapter II.

5. Ibid.

6. The "net figure" refers to the post-2008 cumulative number of restrictive measures less the number of liberalizing measures.

7. Editor's note: a policy of "beggar-thy-neighbor" advances a national economy at the expense of other countries, for example by deliberately maximizing the national trade surplus.

8. Inga Heiland, *Global Risk Sharing Through Trade in Goods and Assets: Theory and Evidence*, CEPR Working Paper 14230, 2021.

9. Dani Rodrik, *The Globalization Paradox: Democracy and the Future of the World Economy* (New York: W.W. Norton & Co., 2011).

10. *The Economist*, "Slowbalisation: The Future of Commerce," January 24, 2019.

11. Gabriel Felbermayr and Guntram Wolff, "Wohin steuert die Weltwirtschaft?" in *Internationale Politik*, (1) 2023, pp. 18–25.

12. Peter Eppinger, Gabriel Felbermayr, Oliver Krebs, and Bohdan Kukharskyy, "Decoupling Global Value Chains," CESifo Working Paper 9079, 2021.

13. Ibid.

14. Aleksandra Kirilakha, Gabriel Felbermayr, Constantinos Syropoulos, Erdal Yalcin, and Yoto V. Yotov, "The Global Sanctions Data Base: An Update that Includes the Years of the Trump Presidency" in Peter A.G. van Bergeijk (ed.), *The Research Handbook on Economic Sanctions* (Cheltenham: Edward Elgar Publishing, 2021).

15. See Harry G. Johnson, "Optimum Tariffs and Retaliation" in *The Review of Economic Studies* 21(2), 1953, pp. 142–53.

16. Blackwill and Harris, *War by Other Means*.

CHAPTER 13

EQUALITY, INEQUALITY, LAW

CHRISTOPH G. PAULUS

THE LAW AS A LEVELER

If we want to locate human beings within the dichotomy of equality and inequality, we must fix the Archimedean point from which we intend to do this, otherwise we're talking at cross-purposes. For example, from a biological perspective, people share a great deal of equality: birth and death form the framework common to every life, and the organs of the body are *grosso mo*♦*o* equally distributed. Theologians too will say that all people are equal before God. By contrast, a sociological perspective will probably always point up inequalities: one person is a highly gifted mathematician, while the other is a talented athlete, and a third is neither one nor the other but a good conversationalist in company. It is, however, hard to determine exactly what the legal perspective is. Nevertheless, in this essay we shall attempt to do so.

First of all, we should identify our starting point for determining the answer in this more limited field as well. This is because when addressing this issue a constitutional lawyer would probably immediately think of the principle of equality that heads the list of fundamental rights, while employment lawyers, for example, would see and point out lots of differences in order to do justice to the range of different professions. And a company lawyer is primarily concerned with associations, while largely ignoring individuals as different from what they deal with. If we approach our present question against this backdrop, we should therefore do so from a historical perspective and begin by specifying whether there is such a thing as a starting point where a uniform situation of equality or inequality existed.

This question implies an adherence either to the ideas of Thomas Hobbes and his famous postulate that a man is a wolf to another man (*homo homini lupus*), or to those of Jean-Jacques Rousseau, according to whom the beginning of human development was characterized by a state of paradise. If, according to Hobbes, the starting point is all-out conflict, this implies inequality, because those who are stronger are confronted by those who are more cunning, for example; while in the work of Rousseau, where lions dwell alongside people and venomous snakes, equality is predominant. As is so often the case, in this alternative too, in which the protagonists are positioned diametrically opposite one another, the middle way is likely to come closest to the truth. This ultimately common-sense thesis is advanced in the book *The Dawn of Everything* by anthropologist David Graeber and archaeologist David Wengrow, according to whom approximations of these opposing ideals have existed at all times, often in close proximity.

In the dim and distant past, the law began with prohibitions. That is at least what is suggested by some of the oldest surviving written documents, in which writing is used to categorically prohibit a certain action. The audience for these writings are all targeted equally. It is of course uncertain when the rules for concluding a contract emerged. But whether this required a certain action in advance (for example, a handshake) or the pronouncement of a certain formula (a promise or a curse directed at oneself), or ultimately conformity between two declarations of intent, offer and acceptance, in any case a generalizing statement was agreed on in such a way that all legal subjects had to conform to this behavior equally if they sought to achieve the specific goal, namely the conclusion of a contract. Of course, these examples represent a plethora of others, from the Ten Commandments of the Old Testament through the Code of Hammurabi to the *Corpus Juris Civilis* issued under the Byzantine Emperor Justinian, not to mention the thousands upon thousands of later codifications and laws.

Let's be clear: the fact that there are and have been exceptions, and that rules have always been and are being broken, does not provide a categorical counterargument to our thesis that the law is in principle a leveler. Anatole France's famous words, "The law, in its majestic equality, forbids rich and poor alike to sleep under bridges, to beg in the streets, and to steal their bread" are, on reflection, castigating not so much the law as social realities.

The leveling nature of the law can be seen in a particularly wonderful and vivid way in an extraordinarily momentous tenet of ancient Roman law, which can be found in the *Digest* as one of the legal rules laid down in the last book of this monumental body of laws:

princeps legibus solutus est [the sovereign is not bound by the laws]. It was this very phrase from the *Digest* that led to the characterization of an entire era in the Early Modern period—absolutism. Its most prominent representative was probably France's King Louis XIV, who was convinced from the bottom of his heart that he and the state were one and the same: *L'état, c'est moi.* And yet, nothing could be more wrong than to want to derive this equation from the original, ancient Roman understanding of the state in the era of the Principate, even if this seems to be what is being expressed in the above-mentioned maxim.

This maxim was isolated and used out of context for the first time in Byzantine legal legislation, around the year 530 CE, at the behest of the above-mentioned Emperor Justinian, and it sums up the power relationships of the time. During this period, too, the prevailing understanding was that every Byzantine ruler was not bound by the laws he had enacted. However, the entire text in which this maxim originally appeared is a good five hundred years older: it was, more precisely, a system of legislation drawn up by Princeps Augustus and which is remarkable for several reasons. In order to replenish the senatorial class, which had been dramatically decimated during the preceding hundred years of civil war, Augustus passed a package of legislation that operates today under the banner of *family legislation*. Enacted around the turn of the millennium, the *leges Papia et Poppea* tried in a variety of ways to create incentives for the upper class to have at least three children. Those who did so were rewarded with benefits and privileges regarding status and inheritance.

Princeps Augustus, the originator of these laws, was not able, despite his best efforts, to meet this criterion; his adopted sons and his daughter all died. For this reason, he decreed *princeps legibus solutus est*—this was not therefore a decision in principle, but just about exemption from the *jus trium liberorum*, i.e., the right of three children. Under these circumstances, it is significant that this exception had to be specifically codified during the period of the Principate. This implicitly expresses the fact that the Princeps himself should not have received the benefits as decreed without a specific legal exemption. Understood in context, what follows from this regulation is the exact opposite of absolutism, namely that the Regent is bound by the laws he has enacted. Only by isolating this regulation, therefore, was it possible to create this major historical impact.

ON THE *EQUALITY* OF STATES

Having already discussed absolutism, it is logical to move to a related issue, namely the legal concept of sovereignty, which implies the equality of states. Developed by the French philosopher Jean Bodin (c. 1530–1596), this legal construct had an enormous impact during the Renaissance, enjoying a further resurgence under the above-mentioned absolutist King Louis XIV. This was because sovereignty not only guaranteed every state's internal freedom to act and its monopoly on the use of force, but also its respective independence. Louis' maxim made it clear that he, the king, was the sovereign.

Although not entirely undisputed, this concept of the sovereignty of each individual state still applies today. One of its effects, for example, is that the vote that countries such as the Seychelles or São Tomé and Príncipe have at the United Nations carries just as much weight as that of the USA, Germany, or Japan. The continued importance of this equality and self-determination can be seen nowhere so clearly and appreciably as in the group of European states, where Brexit was positively fueled by the call for full sovereignty to be restored, and where election campaigns in several countries focus precisely on this goal. In this context, relinquishing sovereign rights is clearly one of the most painful encroachments on any state's right to self-determination.

How justified or contrived these efforts are or may be should not detain us further. Of more interest here are the factual inequalities between countries beyond the obvious differences in size and power between, for example, Belize on the one hand and China on the other. Let us take as an example the phenomenon of migration, which has always existed but has become increasingly pressing in recent years for a variety of reasons. The causes are many and varied: for some time they have been the result of global warming, but for a long time equally the result of the challenges brought about by nation building, which usually go hand in hand with corruption and self-enrichment on the part of the ruling elites. In any case, poverty is a huge problem.

The pandemic and Russia's war against Ukraine have only recently added to this vicious circle. Due to the catastrophic situations around the world, the pandemic led to a massive increase in debt, with the result that the already exorbitant mountain of debt grew immeasurably throughout the world. For many of the poorest countries, attempts at debt reduction that had previously been quite successful suddenly became ineffective and gave way to debt levels that are now often much higher than they have ever been. Adding to this disaster, the war in Ukraine is dramatically increasing the cost of food, energy, and many other basic necessities. And here, too, money is not the solution to the problem, but it is an indispensable medium for alleviating the worst excesses. The result is that the multilateral institutions, above all the Bretton Woods institutions of the International Monetary Fund (IMF) and the World Bank, which otherwise come in for such ready and intense criticism, are increasingly being asked for loans as so-called "lenders of last resort."

Alternatively, or even preferably, individual countries may come up with offers. However, this too can turn out to be disastrous. Whenever an appropriate offer of a loan is received by a head of state or their finance minister, the following principle should be flagged up as a warning signal, a principle that the second President of the United States, John Adams, pronounced more than two hundred years ago: "There are two ways to conquer and enslave a country. One is by the sword. The other is by debt." At present, it is China in particular whose loan offers are occasionally referred to (or branded) at least in the West as "debt-trap diplomacy" (of course some hundred years earlier the US had done something similar with Nicaragua and the Gulf of Fonseca). This kind of diplomacy has resulted in China signing a 99-year lease on a port and an area 15 miles inland in Sri Lanka, to cite just one example among several (India is far from amused by China's seizure). This came about because Sri Lanka, which became officially insolvent in 2022, was a few years ago no longer able to pay off its massive debts towards China, debts that were mainly incurred by building a new port—a construction plan all consultants projected in advance as completely nonsensical from an economic point of view.

Whoever the lender, the loan must be repaid one way or another at some point. In addition to the pandemic-related and war-related plight of many of today's heavily indebted countries, there is also the long-term problem which, at the latest by the time the repayment obligation materializes, leads to what is colloquially referred to as "state bankruptcy." What that means became a little clearer when in 2010 Greece announced that it was on the brink of such a situation. But what is probably less well known is the fact that today, for example, almost all island states in the Caribbean and the South Seas are actually broke—and the reason for this is global warming. As a result of rising water levels, coastlines are disappearing or have to be constantly repaired at great expense in order to save tourism at least as a source of income for these countries. But a look at the past also shows us that there have been over three hundred state bankruptcies in the last 250 years or so, affecting practically every country in the world: Germany has appeared on this list twice in the last century.

We should at this point interrupt our discussion of this catastrophic situation, which can be extended every which way, in order to provide a summary, namely that the equality between states that has been created and postulated by law through the notion of sovereignty may well be reflected in the right to cast a vote at the UN, for example, but not in the reality of everyday (geo-)politics which reveals a situation of absolutely stark inequality. Based on this evidence, therefore, the question we should ask is what can the law do, if not to eliminate the massive inequality we have only hinted at here, then at least in the worst case—that of state bankruptcy—to mitigate it?

RESOLVENCY LAW

In searching for an answer, we first encounter a remarkable piece of evidence that does not enhance the reputation of the legal profession. Even after centuries of experience in this regard, there is no established legal framework for regulating this situation. A dedicated field of the law has not yet emerged to address the phenomenon of state bankruptcy, which has been known since antiquity. This operational blindness has only gradually begun to disappear over the last few years, as such a thing as resolvency law slowly begins to develop. The intention of this term, expressing the opposite of insolvency law, is to clarify that its sole purpose is to guide an over-indebted country back to sustainability. Liquidation, meaning a disposal of assets equivalent to the bankruptcy procedure, is therefore excluded per se and categorically.

In fact, such resolvencies are currently handled largely by conducting negotiations between the debtor state and its creditors. However, because there is no fixed regulatory framework for this, numerous different factors play a more or less clearly identified role in these discussions. The fact that the first official act of Greek Prime Minister Alexis Tsipras, when newly elected in 2015, was a trip to Moscow was, during the still simmering currency crisis of that time, nothing but a signal to the European creditor countries that the south-eastern flank of Europe is a valuable asset for the European Union that is worth saving. Similarly, in the 19th century, the bankruptcies of Egypt and

Turkey, which were basically the same in terms of debt and creditors, each took a completely different course. Egypt controlled the Suez Canal, which at that time was indispensable in terms of economic importance. Turkey could not come up with anything comparable. In short, today as ever, basic conditions exist that may be totally unequal.

An orderly, regulating procedure, a resolvency procedure, would remedy this situation. Such a procedure could bring about equality of treatment which, in combination with transparency, predictability, and calculability, would represent such a thing as the core element of the rule of law. This in turn, especially in Europe, is tantamount to the motto of the Union which is always emphasized and held up. However, the clearly politically motivated resistance to such proposals is immense; even the IMF failed in the attempt. And yet, over the past twenty years or more since the failure of the Sovereign Debt Restructuring Mechanism (SDRM) proposed by the IMF, a very gradual development is emerging that will one day perhaps result in a legally binding resolvency procedure. Through current recommendations above all and the identification of best practices, progress is being made in the direction of so-called "soft law," which according to legal classification is completely non-binding, but which, if only because the word "law" appears in this identification, professes to be more than just a desire or a recommendation.

In other words, the achievement of equality requires hard work. In this respect, the process we have described is indeed paradigmatic for the law's constant efforts to create a level playing field in light of existing real inequalities. However, we should be under no illusions here either: the relationship between creditors and debtors has always been tense and characterized by power struggles. So even if due legal process were to be introduced one day, experience has shown that it will be used strategically after a period of familiarization, which in turn will lead to new inequalities that later theorists and practitioners will have to work out how to eliminate. The law will probably always be playing catch up on the requirement to create or at least pave the way for equality.

Bibliography

Jean Bodin, *Les six livres de la République* (Paris, 1576).

David Graeber and David Wengrow, *Anfänge. Eine neue Geschichte der Menschheit* (Stuttgart: Klett-Cotta, 2021).

Anatole France, *The Red Lily* [1894] (Dodo Press, 2007).

Christoph G. Paulus, "Freiheit und Gleichheit als Grenzmarkierung zwischen Zivilrecht und Insolvenzrecht" in *Perspektiven ꜰes Privatrechts am Anfang ꜰes 21. Jahrhunꜰerts – Festschrift für Dieter Meꜰicus zum 80. Geburtstag*, ed. Volker Beuthien et al. (Cologne: Carl Heymans Verlag 2009), pp. 281 ff.

Christoph G. Paulus, "Warum benötigen wir ein Resolvenzverfahren?" in *Zeitschrift für Wirtschaftsrecht* (ZIP) (Cologne, 2019), pp. 637 ff.

Adam Smith, *An Inquiry into the Nature anꜰ Causes of the Wealth of Nations* (London, 1776).

CHAPTER 14

EQUALITY—FROM POSTULATE TO PROBLEMS

STEFAN KORIOTH

I.

In the early Christian Church a long and bitter dispute took place about the nature of Jesus. Essentially it concerned the relationship between the human and the divine, whether Jesus was similar or equal to God the Father. As is so often the case in Western culture, the substance and consequences of the debate were not just theological.[1] It also had an impact on other areas of culture.

Three aspects are of interest for the problem of equality. First, in the context of ancient philosophy, a whole range of degrees of correlation emerged, ranging from disparateness via similarity and equality to identity. Second, the broad scope of equality's applicability became clear. As a standard and requirement, equality can refer to things, facts, the divine, and the human, and in doing so describes a relationship. Typically, it is about the relationship between at least two people. The relationship is the result of a comparison, in which the people placed in a relationship with each other can compare themselves, or this can be done by a third party. Third, the argument about the nature of Jesus tells us why equality is so important and why it is so bitterly disputed. It is not just about comparing and the result of the comparison. The result of equality or inequality creates a status. This status is not natural or predetermined, but the result of evaluation and assignation. As with all processes of evaluation and assignation, the result can be called into question, the entitlement to equality or inequality can be affirmed or criticized. At the same time, this reveals a difference between freedom and equality. Freedom can be understood as natural and innate, without need for a third party to recognize or assign it. This is not possible in the case of equality. There is no natural equality in the sense that it would be conceivable without reference to others and their recognition of it. Of course, in a second step the differences between freedom and equality level out again. Freedom too is a social phenomenon, requiring respect and mutual recognition. But self-determination is an indispensable part of freedom, while equality through self-determination remains a remarkable pretension that is always in danger of not being accepted by others. One is not equal in one's own right, but in a social context.

The basic human need for equality arises when it comes to communicating status—without a reliable way of determining what equality is or might be. Comparing and determining equality, as well as inequality, superiority, or inferiority, is a permanent basic feature of social action and communication. This also means that alongside the desire for equality, there may also arise the opposing desire to be unequal, to differentiate oneself, but also to be equal despite such inequality. It may even be possible in certain respects to demand or justify inequalities on the basis of equality. This spectrum plays a particular role in the current debate about equality, which is dominated by questions of diversity and parity.

II.

Our investigation into the many levels of equality leads us first to what is traditionally called political equality or equality through (state) citizenship. Every serious political theory recognizes the fundamental principle of equality of every human being and the resulting claim to be treated with the same esteem and respect by everyone else and by public authorities. Since the 18th century, the era when inequalities in all areas of life that were previously considered self-evident were dismantled, this has been an integral part not only of legal theory but also of normative legal texts. Art. 1 of France's *Declaration of the Rights of Man and of the Citizen* of August 26, 1789, says: "Les hommes naissent et demeurent libres et égaux en droits. Les distinctions sociales ne peuvent être fondées que sur l'utilité commune." Art. 6 (2): La loi "doit être la même pour tous, soit qu'elle protège, soit qu'elle punisse." In Germany, Art. 4 of the Prussian Constitution of 1850 stipulated: "All Prussians shall be equal before the law. Class privileges shall not be permitted. Public offices, subject to the conditions imposed by law, shall be uniformly open to all who are competent to hold them." Today's constitutions see equality of rights moreover not only as a status imparted by state citizenship but as a human right: "All persons shall be equal before the law," as stated in Art. 3 (1) of Germany's Basic Law [GG].

The norms of the 18th and 19th centuries did not achieve equal citizenship and legal equality all at once. The establishment of equality of rights required long-term cultural and social processes, but above all changes to the entire legal system, which lasted until well into the 20th century. Equality through state citizenship becomes possible through the law. The means of enshrining equality of rights despite all people's individualities and differences was the well-established concept of the legal person. A person in the legal sense is a construct and not the same as a human being, but it can be applied to both human beings (*natural persons*) and organizations (*juridical persons*). The person is abstracted from all differences and focuses on normative equality, which is understood as the only condition of legal capacity.

III.

Equality through state citizenship is in one respect rooted in and upheld by older debates on moral and philosophical equality. Since antiquity the principle has been that equals should be treated equally for justice to be done. Equality is justice and vice versa. A legal definition that has almost been forgotten today but was significant in post-1945 Germany, shows that this can be realized despite the indeterminacy of equality and justice. In 1945 the victorious Western powers of World War II decided (and after 1949 the West German legislature followed suit) that the laws passed between 1933 and 1945 should continue to apply in principle. At first sight this seems disconcerting, but it was for the good and pragmatic reason of avoiding legal chaos. Above all, however, laws based on Nazi ideology that made a mockery of the elementary principles of justice were excluded from this continued application. In order to identify such laws, after 1945 the courts called on the criterion of equality: laws that went contrary to the principle of equality—today we would say discriminatory laws— could no longer apply. In 1946 Gustav Radbruch summed this up in a well-known formula, which incidentally also regained importance after 1990 in the debate about the East German legal system. According to this formula, even an unjust law is valid "except for cases where the discrepancy between the positive law and justice reaches a level so unbearable that the statute has to make way for justice because it has to be considered 'erroneous law'. [...] Where justice is not even strived for, where equality, which is the core of justice, is renounced in the process of legislation, there a statute is not just 'erroneous law', it is in fact not of a legal nature at all."[2]

On this basis the Federal Republic of Germany's Energy Industry Act of 1935, the amended Stock Corporation Act of 1937 (despite the implementation of the "Führer principle" regarding the powers of the Executive Board), and the Reich Concordat of 1933[3] continued to apply, but by contrast not those laws that disenfranchised and discriminated against individuals and groups of individuals during the Nazi period.[4] Justice is first and foremost equal treatment in formal and schematic terms.

IV.

Currently the most controversial aspect of equality concerns social equality. We can distinguish two stages of development. The first began in the 19th century during the process of fully establishing equality of rights. It did not go unnoticed that this formal equality reduced privileges, but at the same time revealed a blind spot. Formal equality before the law masks the very different basic features and actual life situations of each individual that make it easier or harder for the individual to achieve their own goals in life and actually be able to exercise their freedom. As Anatole France commented sarcastically: "The law, in its majestic equality, forbids rich and poor alike to sleep under bridges, to beg in the streets, and to steal their bread."[5]

In West European welfare states between 1945 and 1990, large-scale programs were therefore created to supplement equality of rights with procedural equality. Historians now see this phase as the welfare state being developed to provide the basis for maintaining the capitalist economic system, which had enjoyed little success and attractiveness during the interwar period. In the name of social justice and by enhancing education and social budgets, the aim was to compensate for undeserved advantages and disadvantages, differences in skills, talents and material starting conditions, and to support the disadvantaged.[6] Today unjustly discredited as utopian, "equal opportunities" was the very mantra of Western democracies in the second half of the 20th century. Anatole France's verdict was ironically summed up by the British rock band The Who in a new and different way in their song *Substitute* (1966). The lyrics are about a man who always came second and who, after a moment's hesitation, acknowledges it and doesn't give up. He sings about the many ways he is pretending to be more than he is and explains that he was born with a "plastic spoon" in his mouth. The rock group from Shepherd's Bush acknowledged that even in the 1960s equality was a promise that wasn't yet fulfilled in reality and wasn't totally fulfillable. It made a difference whether you were born with a plastic or a silver spoon in your mouth.

The second and entirely new stage of development of social equality is a mercurial phenomenon for which no comprehensive term has yet been found. We might call it *material free*♦*om, equality of outcome*, but also *equity* as opposed to *equality*. The point is that more and more reasons for unequal treatment are formally prohibited (or such is the intention) not only for public authorities, but also for all members of society. There are, for example, the comprehensive anti-discrimination clauses in EU law, which in Germany—as in other countries—led to the 2006 General Equal Treatment Act [Allgemeines Gleichbehandlungsgesetz or AGG]. This aims to eliminate or prevent discrimination on grounds of "race or ethnic origin, gender, religion or belief, disability, age or sexual identity."

In such a norm, the general obligation of each legal subject disrupts all conventional categories of public commitment and freedom of self-determination. The relationship between the commitment to equality and freedom of action is being redefined. In light of anti-discrimination norms, the demand for equal treatment is no longer the (exceptional) justification for restricting freedom. In a complete reversal, comprehensive equal treatment is primary, while freedom of action is the choice and options remaining to the individual once all requirements for equality are met. Inverting all models of society since the Enlightenment, freedom becomes the residual function of equality.

How far this way of thinking has now progressed can be seen in a 2018 decision by Germany's Federal Constitutional Court, which concerned a nationwide stadium ban on a violent football fan, which was imposed by a club by virtue of its private "house rules" [*Hausrecht*]. The "central issue" of the case was that "the complainant was treated unequally compared to persons who were granted access to the stadium."[7] This also means that the "central issue" of the dispute is not the club's decision to exclude a potential spectator from access to football matches by virtue of its own (and in this specific case justifiable) decision and the countervailing civil liberties of the excluded individual. Indeed the Court's decision said that the principle of equal treatment in Art. 3 (1) of the Basic Law "does not give rise to an objective constitutional principle according to which legal relationships between private actors would be generally subject to equality guarantees [...] However, under specific circumstances, equality requirements relating to relationships between private actors may arise from Art. 3 (1) GG," for example at major events, "which the organizers, of their own volition, had opened up to a large audience without distinguishing between individual persons," so that an exclusion "has a considerable impact on the ability of the persons concerned to participate in social life." "By undertaking to organize such events, private actors also take on a special legal responsibility under constitutional law."[8] No one should be excluded without factual reasons. The individual will lose its decisive role in shaping private legal relationships. In this case, the organizer also bears "a special legal responsibility under constitutional law [!]. They may [!] not use their discretionary powers, which here result from the right to enforce house rules—in other cases they might potentially arise from a monopoly or a position of structural advantage—to exclude specific persons from such events without factual reasons."[9] In each individual case there can be good or less good reasons for such a comprehensive ban on unequal treatment. For many people, access to commercial football games, for example, may indeed mean participation in social life. However, legal requirements that are based on equality of outcome fundamentally change the relationship between freedom and behavioral requirements based on equality. What the Federal Constitutional Court is ruling here is nothing other than the direct binding effect of the constitutional principle of equality in Art. 3 (1) of the Basic Law on private action. Perhaps here—as in completely different areas as well—a fragmented society is reacting to the loss of shared and extra-legal beliefs about what is right and wrong by creating an inflexible form of juridification. The risk of making excessive demands on and losing control of the law is accepted. But what is even more serious, is that new inequalities are being created, not unconsciously or as a side effect, but completely intentionally. Sometimes it is stated expressly that there must be unequal treatment now to compensate for instances of unequal treatment in the past.

Various so-called "parity laws" provide further examples of this, not in the context of a private law society, but in the context of the process of political decision-making. These laws require, when conducting parliamentary elections, that the political parties submitting lists should fill their lists equally and alternately with men and women. This restricts freedom in drawing up lists and consequently also voters' freedom. The aim is to achieve an arithmetically equal number of men and women in parliament. The courts in Germany have (so far) considered such laws to be incompatible with the principle of free elections, but above all with the principle of universal representation in parliament—each member of parliament and parliament as a whole do not represent the interests of different population groups but the electorate as a whole.[10] In such legal statements, it is less individual freedom of choice and more a classic understanding of parliamentary representation that limits the serious effects of the required equality of outcome. Redress is now being recommended via a constitutional amendment that is intended to ensure that women and men are represented equally in parliament. That would be a further step towards creating freedom of decision and action in a way that is based on equality. These aspects of equality today also have the potential to bring society together or to divide it.

Notes

1. The Nicene Creed summarizes the binding principle thus: Jesus Christ is "the only Son of God, eternally begotten of the Father, God from God, Light from Light, true God from true God, begotten not made, one in being with the Father."

2. Gustav Radbruch, "Gesetzliches Unrecht und übergesetzliches Recht" in *Sü﬇eutsche Juristen-Zeitung* 1, (Tübingen, 1946), pp. 105–08; also in Radbruch, *Rechtsphilosophie*, 8th edn., (1973), pp. 339–45.

3. Decision of the Federal Constitutional Court, BVerfGE 6, 309 (331 f.).

4. Decision of the Federal Constitutional Court, BVerfGE 28, 98 (105 ff.).

5. Anatole France, *The Red Lily* [1894] (Dodo Press, 2007).

6. The appropriate social theory, first presented in 1971, is John Rawls, *A Theory of Justice*, of 1971. Here Rawls presents the principle of difference. Inequality is justifiable in a society if it results in the poorest member of society not being worse off or even better off. Inequality is only sustainable in the interests of the weakest.

7. Decision of the Federal Constitutional Court, BVerfGE 148, 267 (283, note 38). See https://www. bundesverfassungsgericht.de/SharedDocs/Entscheidungen/ EN/2018/04/rs20180411_1bvr308009en.html

8. Decision of the Federal Constitutional Court, BVerfGE 148, 267 (283, note 40 f.). See https://www. bundesverfassungsgericht.de/SharedDocs/Entscheidungen/ EN/2018/04/rs20180411_1bvr308009en.html

9. Decision of the Federal Constitutional Court, BVerfGE 148, 247 (283, note 41). See https://www. bundesverfassungsgericht.de/SharedDocs/Entscheidungen/ EN/2018/04/rs20180411_1bvr308009en.html

10. Latterly, Decision of the Federal Constitutional Court, BVerfG, Decision of the First Chamber of the Second Senate of December 6, 2021 (2 BvR 1470/20); previously Constitutional Court of the State of Brandenburg, Decision of October 23, 2020 (VfGBbg 9/19); Thuringian Constitutional Court, Decision of July 15, 2020 (VerfGH 2/20). See Claus Dieter Classen, "Parité-Gesetze: Frauen sollten Frauen wählen können" in *Zeitschrift für Rechtspolitik* (Munich, 2021), pp. 50–53.

CHAPTER 15

LEADERSHIP IN THE ANTHROPOCENE—RECOGNIZING AND COUNTERACTING INEQUALITIES IN RELATION TO THE NATURAL WORLD

TIMO MEYNHARDT

"Too little too late" is the alarming assessment of the Earth4All initiative regarding the extent and speed with which the major ecological challenges of our time are currently being tackled.[1]

Today the ecological issue is noticeably taking center stage. Natural disasters, the extinction of species, and the increase in extreme weather events make it clear that the climate crisis is no longer something abstract—nobody can turn a blind eye to it. Associated with this are new questions of equality and inequality in the life chances of individuals and the collective. How are burdens shared between different population groups and the generations? Who benefits from social inequalities caused by the climate crisis? And, above all, who loses out?

Exactly fifty years after *The Limits to Growth*, the first report to the Club of Rome, the authors of the Earth4All study, used a system-dynamic computer model to conclude that a "giant leap" is needed to avert irreversible changes on Earth, changes that are leading to ecological and social catastrophes and destroying the physical foundations of human existence. They call for "extraordinary turnarounds" to avoid tipping points beyond which negative developments can no longer be stopped. The melting of the glaciers, the rise in sea levels, or the further weakening of the Gulf Stream are examples of this.

The idea of an *Earth for all* goes hand in hand with the idea that the common good must be thought of in planetary terms today more than ever. This turn-around proposal is nothing less than an attempt to abandon a model for living and economics based on the controllability of the Earth and to search for a new narrative for the habitability of the Earth. At least since the onset of industrialization, the idea of using natural resources effectively and efficiently to increase the quality of life has been dominant, but it is becoming increasingly clear that this approach—which was fraught with conflict from the start—is reaching its limits and going beyond them will result in the destruction of the natural foundations of life.

The price of increasing prosperity by exploiting the Earth system and all its resources might mean being forced into a different way of life and economy. This brings with it an enormous leadership task, which above all requires openness to possible alternatives.

Against this backdrop, new social movements are emerging, climate policy is becoming a central policy area, and the economy is aligning its visions and strategies with the idea of a socio-ecological transformation of capitalism. However, the current approaches are too timid and not just for climate activists—"too little too late" indeed.

In the following essay, after a brief description of a few basic ideas of the Earth4All approach, I would like to draw on the Leipzig Leadership Model to show what leaders and decision-makers can use as a guide when facing the complexity of socio-ecological challenges. In the end it will become clear that the key to change lies first and foremost within ourselves. It

depends on our willingness to recognize an opportunity to reshape our relationship with the natural
world and, in doing so, to draw upon the experiences
of earlier epochs in human history as well.

THE NEED TO TAKE ACTION IN THE INTEREST OF VIABILITY/SURVIVABILITY

Even more clearly than in the study of the limits to
growth, today the focus is on "planetary boundaries,"[2]
i.e., the question of the limits of the safe space in
which human activities can develop without the risk
of unleashing processes in the natural world and the
environment that can severely restrict or even destroy
life on Earth. One example is the melting of the glaciers
as a result of human-induced global warming. Even if
the effects do not manifest themselves in the same way
in all regions and areas, they are triggered by interdependencies on a global scale in which we are all potentially involved.

Nine ecological factors are currently being discussed
in connection with planetary boundaries: climate
change, ocean acidification, stratospheric ozone deple-
tion, atmospheric aerosol loading, biogeochemical
cycles, freshwater consumption, land system change,

biosphere integrity, and the release of novel compounds. If the appropriate load limits are exceeded, according to the hypothesis, the foundations of humanity are at stake. The concept of load limits, originally developed by Earth system and environmental scientists, is by no means limited to ecological factors but is concerned equally with social principles such as peace, social justice, and participation in society.[3]

At this point, it is worth taking a quick look at the concept of load limits. The background is the theory of complex systems and its application to the interaction between human beings and the environment. The starting point is the assumption that humans have an impact on the dynamic balance of nature through their consumption of resources and their behavior, and as a result can alter this balance. If a critical point ("tipping point") and thus a load limit is reached, the system becomes unstable and its behavior unpredictable. It can no longer process the "stress" in the same way as before and cannot return to the old state of equilibrium, but rather reorganizes itself dynamically. In such situations of phase transition, chaotic states can emerge before a new ordered state develops. The decisive factor in the approach to dynamic complex systems is not the constant self-organization of the Earth "system," but the acceptance that human influence has grown significantly since industrialization. The scientific evidence for this is clear and ranges from population growth to environmental pollution and water consumption. "The growth of industrialized societies, largely since the 1950s, has pushed Earth out of the Holocene boundary conditions. We are in unknown territory."[4]

The Earth4All authors are in agreement: "The Earth has entered a new geological epoch: the Anthropocene. This paradigm shift in our understanding of both civilization and the Earth system is as profound as Copernicus's conclusion that Earth orbits the sun or Darwin's theory of natural selection."[5]

The diagnosis of such a fundamental change in basic scientific concepts is—as with the aforementioned paradigm shifts—contentious and the cause of fierce controversies whose outcome is unpredictable. For example, the issue of prioritizing values is obvious when scientific statements of probability are used to justify political measures. The sense of uncertainty is even greater when proposals are made that go far beyond environmental protection in the stricter sense and, at best, have an indirect impact.

However, the body of evidence concerning observable changes is so overwhelming that a simple "business as usual" seems unrealistic. It is irresponsible towards future generations not to include ecological issues in decision-making processes in politics, business, and society. More pressingly, these issues are becoming a question of survival for our modern way of life.

This urgency is increasingly being recognized. In all areas of society, we can see a wide variety of initiatives and innovative approaches that are looking for ways out and alternatives and are not satisfied with a "too little too late" scenario. Bruno Latour and Nikolaj Schultz even describe a new "ecological class" that could form as a group, cutting across ideological camps and becoming involved in new constellations.[6]

It quickly becomes clear how ecological, moral, and political issues are interwoven and influence each other. For example, heatwaves, droughts, heavy rainfall, or rising sea levels affect individual regions and population groups more profoundly than others. As in any process of change, there will be winners and losers and new forms of equality and inequality will emerge, which can be expressed, for example, in access to attractive habitats. Overall, the ecological challenges might become a catalyst for social developments. This is not a new phenomenon in human history. But how can today's forms of society respond successfully to social inequalities in the interests of the common good?

We can see the Earth4All model as an attempt to identify these wider contexts and to understand their interdependencies that will influence our way of life and economy over the coming years. These are systemic challenges that require active intervention and leadership in politics, economics, and civil society.

From an Earth4All perspective, extraordinary turnarounds are needed in five key areas, which are presented in the form of "policy roadmaps."[7] These are geared towards the social structures that can have a major impact on how humans behave as inhabitants of the Earth and how they shape the Earth:

1. Poverty. Low-income countries should adopt new rapid economic growth models that secure well-being for the most vulnerable. A starting point is reform of the international financial system to de-risk and revolutionize investment in low-income countries. *Key policy goals: GDP growth rate of at least 5% per year for low-income countries until GDP is greater than US$15,000 per person per year; the introduction of new indicators for wellbeing.*

2. Inequality. Shocking levels of income inequality must be eliminated. This can be achieved through progressive taxation and wealth taxes, empowering

workers, and dividends from a Citizens Fund. *Key policy goal: The wealthiest 10% take less than 40% of national incomes.*

3. Empowerment of women. Transforming gender power imbalances requires empowering women and investing in education and health for all. *Key policy goal: Gender equity that will contribute to stabilization of world population below nine billion by 2050.*

4. Food. To transform agriculture, diets, food access, and food waste; by 2050 the food system must become regenerative (storing vast volumes of carbon in soils, roots, and trunks) and nature positive. Local food production should be incentivized, and excess inputs of fertilizers and other chemicals significantly reduced. *Key policy goals: Healthy diets for all while protecting soils and ecosystems and not expanding the amount of land, overall, devoted to agriculture; dramatically reducing food waste.*

5. Energy. We must transform energy systems to increase efficiency, accelerate the rollout of wind and solar electricity, halve emissions of greenhouse gases every decade, and provide clean energy to those without. This will also deliver

energy security. *Key policy goal: Halve emissions approximately every ɩecaɩe to reach net zero emissions by 2050.*[8]

It is immediately clear that these turnarounds would involve nothing less than a radical system transformation. This only seems over-ambitious if we assume that there is a viable alternative or forget that the status quo of our current way of life is itself the result of numerous system transformations. The authors are aware that their proposals are to be seen as interventions in highly complex systems that have their own logic and history and whose development cannot be predicted. So, they define so-called "levers" which they expect to have a particularly high impact and which in turn can have an effect on other areas.

In each case they indicate the measures through which the stated goals are to be achieved. In essence, these are aimed at a substantial restructuring of the capitalist mode of production and lifestyles, from the establishment of citizens' funds, revitalization of trade unions, the complete transition to a fossil-free energy system, new growth models, a revolution in agriculture, a change in diet, re-regionalization of trade, financial independence for women and access to leadership positions, universal basic income, and an increased pension, to reforms in the international financial system and a transformation in education.

The authors see what reads as a highly ambitious reform project as a "basis for a new social contract for functioning democracies in the Anthropocene"[9] and as an investment in the future with entrepreneurial opportunities. The crucial idea lies in linking these approaches with the ecological issue. In other words, to prevent the destruction of the physical basis of human life, more and different measures are required than just environmental and animal protection measures. Essentially, then, the ecological issue is not a green question, because answering it covers all areas of life and requires a system transformation precisely with this aim. At this point, opinions differ, because the complexity of the phenomena does not allow us to decide where scientifically proven knowledge ends and where the political influence of experts begins.

I do not want to pursue the question of decision-making in (climate) policy here or question the consistency of the goals themselves. The quality and feasibility of the proposals must be debated through the democratic process and a compromise sought on which priorities to set.

This has also been done for a long time with increasing intensity. In business, it is about the implementation of political guidelines that have been agreed at international level (the UN's Sustainable Development Goals), increased transparency (for example, the EU taxonomy), and new criteria for investments (for example, ESG standards). The ecological transformation is well underway in many companies.

One outstanding example from the political world is the decision of Germany's Federal Constitutional Court concerning the Federal Government's 2019 Climate Protection Act. In its decision, the Court finds the Act to be a violation of fundamental rights, because the distribution of greenhouse gas reduction burdens disadvantages future generations and thus restricts their freedom.[10] This judgment concerning the intertemporal guarantee of freedom is a new phenomenon in the history of the Federal Constitutional Court, and it can be interpreted as signaling a paradigm shift. There has now even been the suggestion of an ecological constitutional framework.[11]

Overall, this clearly shows how previous ways of thinking can be changed under pressure of circumstances. But how can the changing context of entrepreneurial activity be translated into the day-to-day work of leadership? How can we imagine such a combination?

ACCEPTING THE CHALLENGES OF LEADERSHIP

In uncertain circumstances, no one can reliably assess the effects and impacts of their own actions. It makes sense, therefore, to see yourself as part of a greater whole and to focus on your own contribution. Unlike focusing purely on outcomes and results, it is about getting involved to the best of your knowledge and belief, knowing that progress can only be controlled to a limited extent.

Instead of capitulating in the face of the challenge ("There's nothing you can do anyway") or suppressing it ("It won't be that bad"), leadership can be measured by taking responsibility for a contribution—no matter how small it may be. The more complex the challenge, the more good leadership is defined by a contribution to the greater whole (the common good). What part of the challenge is mine? In what way can I get involved? The question of one's own contribution becomes a key question for every leader, because if you want to lead, you have to contribute.

It is this understanding of the role of good leadership that underpins the Leipzig Leadership Model and makes it possible to establish a connection between the major challenges and one's own actions in everyday life (Fig. 1).[12]

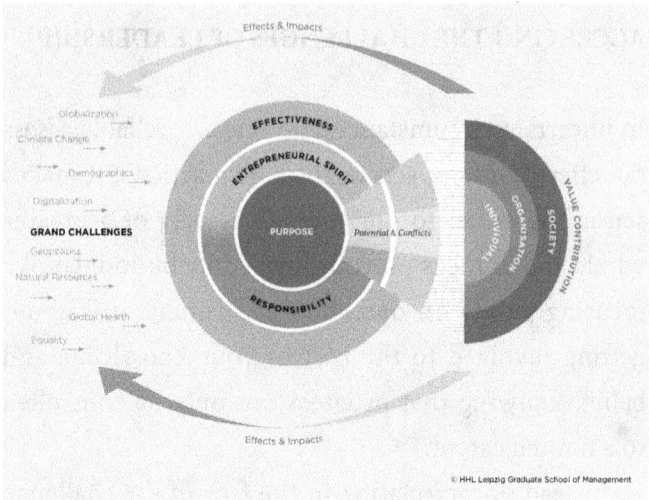

Fig. 1: *The Leipzig Leadership Model*

Between the (internal) acceptance of the challenges and one's own added value resides the work of leadership which, the Model argues, should be based on four core dimensions: purpose, entrepreneurial spirit, responsibility, and effectiveness.

1. The *Purpose* dimension emphasizes the ends–means relationship in leadership. On the one hand, there is the question of "why," the meaning and purpose of leadership decisions. On the other hand, there is the question of "to what end," the contribution to the greater whole. A purpose only emerges by combining both elements to create a motivating

promise of value that goes beyond the company's previous mission and vision.

2. In the *Entrepreneurial Spirit* dimension, the focus is on the ability to renew people, organizations, and society. It is about the very ability to act, create, and innovate. The resulting entrepreneurial spirit not only determines the success of start-ups but also plays an increasingly important role for established private and public companies in processes of transformation.

3. The *Responsibility* dimension is a condition restricting the pursuit of the respective purpose. It is about taking reasonable account of the legitimate expectations of society or, more precisely, of the stakeholders concerned in everyday (leadership) life, and that means above all not disadvantaging anyone unless there are legitimate reasons for doing so. What is feasible and desirable is not always what is responsible, and also the end does not justify the means.

4. The *Effectiveness* dimension deals with the question of the viable or correct path to take in an efficient way. Every purpose needs to be implemented

in a technically and methodically competent way given current and future conditions of scarce resources, competition and, last but not least, legal requirements. The development of goal-oriented strategies, structures, and processes is a basic prerequisite for good leadership.[13]

Using these four perspectives, leadership challenges can be analyzed and evaluated step by step. In other words, dealing with this makes the courses of action more concrete, namely the means and consistency by which an approach to leadership can be pursued.

In many situations, this frame of reference makes it possible to identify areas of tension in the first place, but also to recognize the kinds of potential associated with a decision or action. Above all, the appropriate kind of reflection prevents the viewpoint from becoming too restricted. For example, it is unclear whether exceeding (planetary) load limits in one area will actually have positive effects in other areas. The relevant point of the work of leadership in the paradigm of the Anthropocene is the willingness to adapt to the concept of load limits, to think in the form of dynamic processes, and to determine one's own contribution to the socio-ecological transformation from that position.

In the Model's most recent update[14] to include systemic aspects of feedback and dependency on the greater whole, the complex preconditions of a production system that enable the system in the first place are examined even more closely. This is intended to draw attention to actual effects and realistic impact targets. "Effects" aim to identify unintended influences while "impacts" identify intended influences of entrepreneurial activity on the social environment and the natural world. In the Model, this notion was previously linked to its contribution to the greater whole in terms of social value (the common good) and is now in the expanded Model linked more directly with the Grand Challenges. The Challenges drive the common good, so to speak, which can no longer be brought about without socio-ecological transformation.

As a result, the Model calls for thinking that takes account of cycles, dependencies, and a greater sensitivity to context. In other words, it is a pragmatic way of finding routes that do not formulate the ecological issue as a problem of compensation or reparation, but rather promote a new understanding of consumption, material prosperity, and a sustainable quality of life. The challenge is to avoid solutions (however innovative they may seem) that reproduce the very problems that need to be overcome. For example, why should those who created the problems to begin with be those who are in a position to solve these problems? In general, caution is required if the effects and impacts of entrepreneurial activities are to be assessed.

An interim conclusion: in the Leipzig Leadership Model, a frame of reference has been developed that makes focusing on a company's social function and role the linchpin of good leadership. In this respect, it seems appropriate to address the complex embedding of entrepreneurial activities in a more comprehensive context. In the Anthropocene, this is characterized particularly by the ecological issue, the answer to which can no longer be found solely in the previous logic of our economic system. The Earth4All model provides one suggestion, and its translation into the concrete framework of entrepreneurial activity can be given a systematic structure through the Leipzig Leadership Model: the most demanding purpose comes to nothing if it is not implemented effectively, entrepreneurially, and responsibly. Conversely, in practice it is often hard to set activities in a wider context and to recognize one's own contribution to the greater whole. Good leadership today includes doing both: thinking in terms of the challenges of the Anthropocene and making relevant contributions visible as well as being judged by them. As a reality principle, it is important to constantly reflect on and reassess the possibilities and limits of one's own actions.

GETTING STARTED

To gain insight into the role of the economy in this socio-ecological transformation requires experiences of becoming aware of one's own vulnerability and finiteness in the context of personal development. Today, "inner work" is an important part of leadership coaching because it is seen as a prerequisite for the ability to undergo external transformation.

Such a change in consciousness is certainly prompted by external conditions and can be accelerated by them. At the same time, we should not harbor any illusions that the need to take action will inevitably lead to a collective understanding of the necessity, primarily because the rationality of scientific knowledge is not self-enforcing and the idea of progress itself is constantly being questioned.

The idea of the "turnaround" in the Earth4All approach presupposes an optimism that developments in society can be directly influenced, which is hard to justify from a historical point of view. A system change can neither be mandated nor implemented according to plan. Rather we should assume systemic-evolutionary developments that are difficult to predict and are full of surprises. The authors of the Earth4All model know this too and therefore prefer to speak of scenarios whose likely occurrence differ. They point to paths of development, the recognition of which can lead to more conscious decision-making and reasoning.[15]

With the emerging dominance of the ecological issue, it is not just the modern idea of progress, the notion of making the world controllable through scientific rationality, that is called into question. Today, the visible and foreseeable changes in our natural environment show how dependent we are on it and how we influence it through our actions. A new basic approach might include granting nature its own legal status with rights of self-defense such as individual people have, in the spirit of Bruno Latour's "parliament of things."[16] When people understand themselves to be part of nature again, this changes the notion of nature's ability to be shaped.

The current situation is less about controllability and more about the habitability of the planet. This does not have to be seen as losing possibilities of taking action, but as opening up new opportunities.

"This mood makes itself felt everywhere, politically, socially, and philosophically. We are living in what the Greeks called the *kairos*—the right time—for a 'metamorphosis of the gods,' i.e., of the fundamental principles and symbols." David Graeber and David Wengrow begin their book, *The Dawn of Everything: A New History of Humanity*,[17] with this quotation by C. G. Jung. In this book, which has received many international awards, the authors describe a new image of humanity's past, of different social structures, economic systems, and ways of life. We begin to see the variety of possible forms of human coexistence that changes our understanding of historical processes. In this description, there is no evidence of clear logical progress from "primitive" hunters and gatherers to the present-day, modern way of life. Rather, we come to recognize a constant experimentation, discarding, discovering, and sometimes rediscovering of ways of living together in the community and with nature. This applies to all areas of life: the role of technology, the question of forms of ownership, the relationship with nature, with life and death, dealing with hierarchy and participation, etc. Quintessentially, the book is about relativizing our level of civilization in relation to earlier epochs of human history. Indigenous cultures in particular were much better able to live in harmony with and respect for nature.

By using the *kairos* quotation, Graeber and Wengrow want to point out that, at least in Western societies, a radical change could once more be imminent, which in view of humanity's history hitherto, however, need not frighten us. What is new about today's situation is the unsettling ecological issue, as preserving the very foundations of life depends on our response to it. It doesn't seem too outlandish to talk about a new phase of experimentation and discovery.

Earth4All's alarming assessment of "Too little too late" regarding how to deal with the ecological issue is to be understood as a call to first answer the question of where one's own problem lies, in order to then explore what one's own contribution to new solutions might be. However, the turnarounds that we have discussed must also prove to be practicable and translate into concrete leadership work, as we argued using the example of the Leipzig Leadership Model. This then acts a kind of filter in the deliberation process.

No one can demand that leaders focus on the major challenges all the time in everyday business. However, we can ask that they show willingness to face these questions as reflective practitioners and locate their own actions in this context.

Leadership in the Anthropocene means helping oneself and others in an effective way to find a new approach to nature and life in general. Without an inner willingness to think of one's own existence in terms of its dependence on others and the natural environment, the ecological issue remains at best a technique to be mastered for optimizing resource consumption and smart offsetting. It would be a mistake by other means to see the solution to these problems only in more innovation. It is more sustainable to see oneself as a resident with responsibility for the home we share. It is not enough if people see themselves as part of nature but attribute a separate value to it. The crucial step is the recognition of nature's agency. Only then can inequalities in relation to nature be suitably addressed.

It will be interesting to see how the regulatory interventions expected over the next few years in favor of making the economy and society greener will change practices. In the Anthropocene, good leadership also means recognizing and being able to counteract new (social) inequalities.

Notes

1. Sandrine Dixson-Declève, Owen Gaffney, Jayati Ghosh, Jorgen Randers, and Johan Rockström, *Earth for All. A Survival Guie for Humanity* (Gabriola BC, Canada: New Society Publishers, 2022).

2. Johan Rockström et al., "Planetary Boundaries: Exploring the Safe Operating Space for Humanity" in *Ecology an* Society 19 (2), 2009.

3. Kate Raworth, *Doughnut Economics: Seven Ways to Think Like a 21st-Century Economist* (New York: Random House Business, 2017).

4. Dixson-Declève et al., *Earth for All*, p. 15.

5. Dixson-Declève et al., *Earth for All*, p. 13.

6. Bruno Latour and Nikolaj Schultz, *On the Emergence of an Ecological Class. A Memo*, trans. Julie Rose (Cambridge: Polity Press, 2022).

7. Dixson-Declève et al., *Earth for All*, p. 5.

8. Dixson-Declève et al., *Earth for All*, p. 20 f.

9. Dixson-Declève et al., *Earth for All*, p. 22.

10. See https://www.bundesverfassungsgericht.de/SharedDocs/ Entscheidungen/EN/2021/03/rs20210324_1bvr265618en. html (accessed January 30, 2023).

11. Jens Kersten, *Das ökologische Grun* gesetz (Munich: C.H. Beck, 2022).

12. Timo Meynhardt, Manfred Kirchgeorg, Andreas Pinkwart, Andreas Suchanek, and Henning Zülch (eds.), *Führen in* *er Krise: Herausfor* erungen an *as Leipziger Führungsmo* ell (Leipzig: HHL Academic Press, 2022).

13. Ibid., p. 18 f.

14. In the first version of 2017, the systemic perspective with the idea of value contribution at various levels in the system (individual, organization, society) was already in place and was reflected in the theoretical frame of reference. In the expanded version of 2022, the list of Grand Challenges was updated and the feedback to the Challenges concretized in the form of unintended effects and intended impacts.

15. The model used for Earth4All is based partly on the model that was used in the study *The Limits to Growth.* The scenario developed in the latter, "Business as Usual," turned out in retrospect to be very realistic (cf. Dixson-Declève et al., *Earth for All*, p. 11).

16. Bruno Latour, *Politics of Nature: How to Bring the Sciences into Democracy*, trans. Catherine Porter (Cambridge, MA: Harvard University Press, 2004).

17. David Graeber and David Wengrow, *The Dawn of Everything: A New History of Humanity* (New York: Penguin, 2022).

CHAPTER 16

ARCHITECTURE FOR A GLOBAL COMMUNITY

HANS ULRICH OBRIST AND DIÉBÉDO FRANCIS KÉRÉ IN CONVERSATION

An edited transcript of a conversation between Hans Ulrich Obrist and Francis Kéré at the Convoco Forum on July 30, 2022 in Salzburg

Hans Ulrich Obrist: I am incredibly happy to welcome Francis Kéré. When Corinne Flick and I started talking about the theme "Equality in an Unequal World," it was from the very beginning our dream to have Francis here with us in Salzburg. Francis and I met many years ago, thanks to the late Christoph Schlingensief, the visionary artist, social sculptor, filmmaker, and writer. Christoph was Francis' first German client and invited him to do the Opera Village.

Francis and I got to know each other very well when we worked on the Serpentine Pavilion in 2017. The Serpentine Pavilion is an annual architecture commission. It has free admission, which is important to us as it means that it is fully accessible not only for people who come to see it but also for passersby—those who maybe would never intend to visit but just stumble across it and have a transformational experience. Francis' pavilion was inspired by the tree that serves as a central meeting point of life in Francis' hometown Gando. It was a very responsive pavilion to connect its visitors to nature. Saskia Sassen, the eminent sociologist who talked about the importance of spaces where we can restore ourselves, said that Francis had created a space of indeterminacy where one can freely invent how to use the structure. This aspect of participation is always central in Francis' work.

Francis' trajectory as an architect began with the building of an amazing school. Generosity has always been part of his practice as well as his intention to create the quality that we need to improve people's lives. Today, his work has expanded beyond school buildings in African countries to include structures in Denmark,

Germany, Italy, Switzerland, the UK, and the United States. There are also two incredible parliament buildings which we are going to talk about, a concept for the National Assembly of Burkina Faso in Ouagadougou and the commissioned Benin National Assembly in Porto Novo. Francis is also a professor and has been teaching for many years at the Technical University of Munich. He has recently been awarded the Pritzker Prize, the biggest prize in architecture. It is the first time in 44 years that an African architect has received this prize. Considering the inequality of such prizes is particularly relevant in relation to our theme. For example, we may think of the fact that the Nobel Prize for literature has never been awarded to an extraordinary writer such as the Kenyan Ngũgĩ wa Thiong'o.

The Indian philosopher and economist Amartya Sen famously stated at the beginning of his book *Inequality Reexamined*: "The central question in the analysis and assessment of equality is, I argue here, 'equality of what?' […] A common characteristic of virtually all the approaches to the ethics of social arrangements, which have actually stood the test of time, is to want equality of something."[1] In Francis' work this "something" has been equality of education since the very beginning. That is also what French economist Thomas Piketty writes about in *A Brief History of Equality* (2021). He emphasizes that the main force pushing towards the reduction of inequality has always been the diffusion of knowledge and education. This brings us to Francis' very first project, which in my opinion is one of the 20 most important buildings in the world.

Francis Kéré: Thank you, Hans. Originally, I come from Burkina Faso, a very poor country. I moved to Germany because I got a scholarship to be trained as a carpenter. When I arrived in Germany, it felt like being in a *Schlaraffenlan*, as you'd say in German, a sort of "paradise." Education was free and accessible to everyone. I decided to attend night school in Berlin while during the day I was working to earn money. I finished school after five years and then started to study architecture. Two years into university, I had the feeling that I was very privileged. I was amazed that I could put my imagination onto paper. So, I decided to return to Burkina Faso. My intention was to give something back to my country. When I was seven years old, I had to leave my home because there was no school in my village of Gando. Therefore, I went back to Gando to build schools.

I was still a student when I built my very first school, which was made out of clay. I had to raise money in order to be able to fulfill my mission. Sadly, I had only small funds. Therefore, I got the people to be part of the construction, even women. It just occurred during the process. I didn't come up with this great idea to get the community involved, "participation" was already a slogan in architecture, something existing in my tradition. Today, I am no longer needed at some of my construction sites because I have a huge team. Instead, I am here talking to you. The school project has paved a career.

HUO: You invented many things with this first school building. The building has a different way of fresh air coming in. Can you talk about that?

FK: Yes. The building is in a place where you have only few resources. Having studied in Germany, I had to face the reality that Burkina is a poor place. It was clear to me that when we have no resources, we need our imagination to make use of what we have. When seeing the school, you will ask yourself: "Where is the air-con?" But there is no air-con. I invented the principle of a double-roof system to create natural, passive ventilation.

One could say the whole project was an experiment, but it worked out. Not even six months after the building was finished, almost the entire village wanted to send their kids to school. I had to raise money in Germany to create extension after extension. Then suddenly housing for teachers was needed as they wanted to stay in the village instead of going to the city. Today, more than 1,000 students are in education there.

HUO: Let's talk about another project of yours: the Opera Village. When Christoph Schlingensief, who commissioned the work, told me about it for the first time, it sounded like a utopia—a utopia being gradually built. But one thing is still missing. Can you tell us about it?

FK: The idea for the village was to grow like an organic system, like a spiral. Unfortunately, the opera at the heart of the village is still missing. The center has yet to be built as we didn't have the resources. Once we do, we will add more structures. Christoph's artistic idea behind it is very powerful. I can't stress enough how important it is to connect with artists. If we listen carefully, it can push us to another level. When Christoph came to me with the idea, we faced a lot of criticism. Opera was seen as a Western concern. But his idea was to try and find a way to translate a universal idea to a poor place. Christoph wanted to create a space where artists can meet, and where people from the surrounding areas can have access to education and healthcare facilities. He added a portion of great artistic vision. The project is now one of the most visited sites in Burkina Faso. Every new foreign ambassador coming to Burkina will visit the site within a month. As an architect, I sometimes feel ashamed that we couldn't do more. But as a vision, the Opera Village is working. We have school classes for more than a hundred kids and artists are coming to perform outside. It's a big success. And don't forget— we did all the construction by training locals and using clay from the site.

Following the success of the schools, we thought about the Massachusetts Institute of Technology. Some clients asked: "Why don't you create such a university in Burkina Faso?" I thought to myself: "Wow, we've been struggling to finish a classroom, and now you're dreaming about an MIT." But I quickly realized that these people were aware of the lack of opportunities in this place. As an architect, I love to experiment, and so we really did build a so-called Burkina Institute of Technology. Give me rebars, give me sand, give me mud, give me wood, and I will create. That is what learned to do in Germany. I am convinced it is going to be one of the leading schools in Africa. Talent is equally distributed around the planet, including Africa, but in some places opportunities are missing.

I was born very poor as the first son of a traditional leader. But I had the opportunity to go to school. With the schools and structures that I'm building I want to open more opportunities for young people.

HUO: You continue to develop schools in many countries. But of course, there are lots of other projects.

FK: A restaurant in the National Park in Mali, for example, is a wonderful project. It is a place where people can meet to have discussions at a time in Mali that is full of conflict. As an architect, it's wonderful to have everyone around your project. It is very inclusive: there is a five-star restaurant at the top, but on the lower part you can have good tea for 10 cents.

Another project was designed for the Coachella Festival in the USA in 2019. The organizers wanted me to create sculptures that would play a role of orientation for the visitors. I decided to create giant baobab trees for Coachella. I love baobabs, as in the southern landscape they're a place where one can encounter other people. People meet in their shade. The finished work is the biggest open-sky sculpture in the USA, and it's built using only two materials: plywood and rebar. The sculpture is now serving a poor community in Indio.

Then there is the Xylem Pavilion in Montana, USA. The clients for this project wanted to have a pavilion for their visitors. Even in a rich country like the US, my approach is to have a look around and see what materials I can work with. So, I decided to create a pavilion using US skills and wooden logs, as the US have a lot of natural wood. I combined these resources with my design and—as is the role of an architect today—created the added value that the pavilion doesn't need additional energy, as it is open and well ventilated. It's impressive to see what one can do using very simple materials. It is so important that everyone uses the materials and resources available to them to create. We can create a strong global community when we respond to local availabilities and capacities.

Of course, today I'm talking to you as a very privileged person. I started as someone who builds schools, but now I see myself facing giant projects like the parliament house in Benin. The design in Benin is inspired by the palaver tree. In our tradition this is where we gather, create, and talk about problems.

HUO: You said that you wanted to create an open structure for the parliament in Benin, that you wanted it to be for everyone.

FK: In contrast to the buildings inherited from the colonial past, which were built with high walls to protect the decision-makers and their fake political system, I wanted to create a public gathering space. That is always the goal for my public buildings. They should be walkable and accessible at any time. In this way, I hope political leaders will be forced to make the right decisions. This idea is also behind my earlier concept for the Burkina Faso National Assembly. In 2014 there was a revolution in Burkina because its president of 30 years decided to change the constitution, making him president for life. In response, the people burned down the parliament house.

HUO: But then a self-organized group of artists and politicians approached you...

FK: ...asking me to design a new parliament. The building was to be strong, transparent, include a museum, and be a memorial for the people who have been killed there. A big project. Imagine the difficult position I was in: I'm living in Germany, suddenly being faced with a big commission in Burkina Faso. I am very well known in Burkina Faso, and so the pressure I was put under was immense. The people said: "Our country is in struggle, and we want to create a national project." And so they called their famous son. If I had refused to come, I would have destroyed my reputation—and that may even be true for my tribe. People would have claimed that my tribe does not want to be part of the nation because its son refuses the commission. I was condemned to do the project.

So, I ended up creating a huge pyramid. My hope was that people would say, "Mr. Architect, this is nice, but these are dreams we cannot afford," so that I could go back to Berlin and just keep doing my work. But first, I had to go and present the idea to the president of the parliament house. I expected him to say, "You dreamer, you don't know our reality. You cannot design something like this." But instead, he looked at it and said, "Mr. Architect, I love your project very much, but you have to make it *bigger* for our nation."

I went back to Berlin, where my team was waiting for me to celebrate the rejection of the project. I had to tell them, "No, we have to work hard now!" And often you do these types of projects with no compensation. The good thing about it is that the concept was well received, leading even *The Guardian* newspaper to dig deeper into Burkina Faso's history, the revolution, and the struggle of its people. In this sense, architects are almost like artists. An unbuilt project can be more relevant than any other, generating a lot of other projects in Africa—for example, the parliament house in Benin, which is now under construction.

HUO: Let's end on your most recent project at the Triennale Milan. You did installations and a little tower for the exhibition.

FK: Yes. The exhibition is about "unknown unknowns," which is a political expression. It used to be a philosophical concept, and then US Secretary of Defense Donald Rumsfeld popularized it when using it to explain the war in Iraq. The Triennale decided to explore the world of these "unknown unknowns," now that we're facing COVID and all these other issues. Being part of this, and being a curator and designer, I just wanted to create a symbol. We are facing a lot of problems, and often we get frustrated and run away. We forget to think or to breathe. Therefore, to enter the tower, I wanted the visitors to have to go really low. You basically have to be on your knees—which is great for Europeans as they don't do this often. Once you are inside the tower, you lift yourself up and you see paintings. And the more you lift your head, the more you discover these paintings which end in an opening at the top. Suddenly you are faced with the sky, with yourself, or your community. The idea behind it is just, let us dream big. Between us and the sky, there is so much space. Who would have thought that we found a vaccine against COVID?

I am in architecture to create comfort for those that have nothing, for those who are under-served. At the same time, I want to push those that may have everything to even think about saving others. No matter where you are from—Djibouti, Ukraine, Russia, or China—what will happen in one place will affect all of us.

Note

1. Amartya Sen, *Inequality Reexamine* (Cambridge, MA: Harvard University Press, 1995), p. IX.

CONTRIBUTORS

Prof. Dr. Marietta Auer studied law, philosophy, and sociology at the University of Munich and Harvard University. She completed both the first and second state legal examinations in 1995 and 1997, received her doctorate in law in 2003 and her MA in philosophy and sociology in 2008. She completed her postdoctoral qualification in 2012 and was granted the professorial teaching qualification for civil law, philosophy of law, commercial and corporate law, comparative law, as well as European private law (all at the University of Munich). She received her LLM in 2000 and her SJD in 2012 from Harvard University. In 2001 she received her license to practice as Attorney-at-Law in New York, USA. From 2013 to 2020 she held the Chair of Civil Law and Philosophy of Law at the University of Giessen, and from 2016 to 2019 she served as Dean of the Law Faculty. Since 2020 she has been the Director of the newly established Department for Multidisciplinary Theory of Law at the Max Planck Institute for Legal History and Legal Theory (formerly Max Planck Institute for European Legal History) (Frankfurt am Main) and is Professor of Private Law as well as the International and Interdisciplinary Foundations of Law at the University of Giessen. She has received numerous distinctions and awards, among them the University of Munich Law Faculty Award (2004), Juridical Book of the Year (2005, 2015), Teaching Excellence Award at Bavarian Universities (2006), the Berlin-Brandenburg Academy of Sciences and Humanities Prize for Outstanding Research in the Area of the Foundations of Law and Economy (2017) and was a Fellow at the Berlin Institute for Advanced Study (2019–20). In 2022 she was awarded the Gottfried Wilhelm Leibniz Prize of the German Research Foundation (DFG). Memberships in professional associations and advisory boards as well as evaluation activities, including the expanded Board of the Association of Lecturers in Private Law (Zivilrechtslehrervereinigung e.V.), the Board of Trustees of the Bucerius Law School, the Research Council of the European University Institute, Florence, as well as the Senate and Grants

Committees on Research Training Groups for the German Research Foundation.

Sir Paul Collier is Professor of Economics and Public Policy at the Blavatnik School of Government, University of Oxford, and a Director of the International Growth Centre, and the ESRC research network, Social Macroeconomics. His research covers the transformation from poverty to prosperity; state fragility; the implications of group psychology for development; migration and refugees; urbanization in poor countries and the crisis in modern capitalism, which is the subject of his most recent book, *The Future of Capitalism*. Sir Paul received a knighthood in 2014 for services to promoting research and policy change in Africa and has been listed as one of the hundred most influential public thinkers.

Prof. Gabriel Felbermayr, Ph.D. is Director of the Austrian Institute of Economic Research (WIFO) and a Professor at the Vienna University of Economics and Business. After studying economics and trade at the University of Linz, he went to Florence to pursue his doctoral studies. From 2004 to 2005, he was an Associate Consultant with McKinsey & Co. in Vienna. From 2005 to 2008, he was Assistant Professor at the

University of Tübingen. From 2009 to 2010, he held a Chair in International Economics at the University of Hohenheim (Stuttgart). From 2010 to 2019, he led the ifo Center for International Economics at the University of Munich, where he also served as Professor of International Economics. From 2019 to September 2021, he was President of Kiel Institute for the World Economy. At the same time, he held a Chair in Economics and Economic Policy at Kiel University (CAU). Gabriel Felbermayr is a member of the Scientific Advisory Board of the Germany Federal Ministry for Economic Affairs and Climate Action, and the Chairman of the Statistics Council at Statistics Austria. He is Associate Editor at the *European Economic Review*. Gabriel Felbermayr's research focuses on issues of international trade theory and policy, labor market research, European economic integration, and current economic policy issues. He has published a large number of papers in international scholarly journals, policy briefs, and newspapers. His research has been recognized with various awards.

Prof. Francisco H. G. Ferreira, Ph.D. is the Amartya Sen Professor of Inequality Studies at the London School of Economics, where he is also Director of the International Inequalities Institute. Francisco is an economist working on the measurement, causes and consequences of inequality and poverty in developing countries, with a special focus on Latin America. His work has been published widely and been awarded various prizes, including the Richard Stone Prize in Applied Econometrics and the Kendrick Prize from the International Association for Research in Income and Wealth. He is also an Affiliated Scholar with the Stone Center at the City University of New York; a non-resident Research Fellow at the Institute for the Study of Labor (IZA, Bonn); and currently serves as President of the Latin American and Caribbean Economic Association (LACEA). Prior to joining the LSE, Francisco had a long career at the World Bank, where his positions included Chief Economist for the Africa Region and Senior Adviser in the Research Department. He has also taught in the faculties of Economics at the Pontifícia Universidade Católica do Rio de Janeiro and at the Paris School of Economics. He was born and raised in São Paulo, Brazil, and holds a Ph.D. in Economics from the London School of Economics.

Dr. Corinne Michaela Flick studied both law and literature, taking American studies as her subsidiary, at Ludwig Maximilian University, Munich. She gained her Dr. Phil. in 1989. She has worked as in-house lawyer for Bertelsmann Buch AG and Amazon.com. In 1998 she became General Partner in Vivil GmbH und Co. KG, Offenburg. She is Founder and Chair of the Convoco Foundation. As Editor of Convoco! Editions she has published among others: *How much Freedom must we Forgo to be Free?* (Convoco! Editions 2022), *New Global Alliances: Institutions, Alignments and Legitimacy in the Contemporary World* (Convoco! Editions 2021), *The Standing of Europe in the New Imperial World Order* (Convoco! Editions, 2020), *The Multiple Futures of Capitalism* (Convoco! Editions, 2019), *The Common Good in the 21st Century* (Convoco! Editions, 2018), *Authority in Transformation* (Convoco! Editions, 2017), *Power and its Paradoxes* (Convoco! Editions, 2016), *To Do or Not To Do—Inaction as a Form of Action* (Convoco! Editions, 2015), *Dealing with Downturns: Strategies in Uncertain Times* (Convoco! Editions, 2014).

Prof. Dr. Dr. h.c. Clemens Fuest (b. 1968) is President of the ifo Institute–Leibniz Institute for Economic Research at the University of Munich e.V., Executive Director of CESifo GmbH, Professor of Economics and Public Finance at Ludwig Maximilian University, Munich, and Director of the Center for Economic Studies (CES) at LMU.

He is among other posts a member of the Advisory Board to the German Federal Ministry of Finance and the Franco-German Board of Economic Experts, the European Academy of Sciences and Arts, as well as the Advisory Board of Ernst & Young GmbH. He is a member of the Scientific Advisory Board of the Market Economy Foundation (Kronberger Kreis) and the Foundation for Family Businesses in Germany and Europe. From August 2018 to August 2021 he was President of the IIPF (International Institute of Public Finance e.V.). In 2013 he received the Gustav Stolper Award of the Verein für Socialpolitik (Social Policies Society, VfS), and in 2019 he received the Hanns Martin Schleyer Award for 2018. In 2017 Clemens Fuest received an honorary doctorate from the Karlsruhe Institute of Technology (KIT). His research areas are economic and financial policy, international taxation, tax policy, and European integration. Before his appointment at Munich, he was a professor at the Universities of Cologne (2001–08), Oxford (2008–13), and Mannheim (2013–16). He is the author of a number of books and has published many commentaries and byline articles on contemporary questions of economic policy in national and international journals. He also writes for newspapers such as *Handelsblatt, Frankfurter Allgemeine Zeitung, Die*

Zeit, Sü✦✦eutsche Zeitung, WirtschaftsWoche, Financial Times, and *The Wall Street Journal.*

Prof. Rajshri Jayaraman, Ph.D. is an associate professor of economics and academic director of the FUTURE Institute for Sustainable Transformation at ESMT Berlin. A development and labor economist, her research is largely focused on how economic policy and organizational design can improve economic outcomes and foster social inclusion, especially among the poor and disadvantaged. Her work has been published in leading economics journals including the *American Economic Review* and the *Journal of Political Economy.* Raji holds a Ph.D. in Economics from Cornell University, a MA in International & Development Economics from Yale University, and a BA (Jnt. Honors) in Economics & Finance from McGill University. In addition to her position at ESMT, she holds a faculty appointment at the University of Toronto, and prior to joining ESMT in 2007, she worked at the University of Munich. At ESMT, where she is featured regularly on the Honor Roll for Teaching Excellence, she teaches Data Analytics and Sustainability-related courses.

Diébédo Francis Kéré is an internationally renowned Burkinabè architect and the 2022 Laureate of the Pritzker Architecture Prize. He is recognized for his pioneering approach to design and sustainable modes of construction. His vocation to become an architect comes from a personal commitment to serve the community he grew up in, and a belief in the transformative potential of beauty.

In 2004 his very first building—the Gando Primary School, which he designed, raised funds for, and realized in collaboration with the residents of his hometown while still a student at the Technical University of Berlin—was awarded the prestigious Aga Khan Award for Architecture. In 2005 he founded his architectural practice, Kéré Architecture GmbH, as well as the Kéré Foundation e.V., a non-profit organization that pursues projects in Gando. Since then, Kéré has gone on to become one of the world's most distinguished contemporary architects. Inspired by the particularities of each project's locality and its social tapestry, he and his team work on projects across four continents.

Underpinning his architectural work are his past and present teaching engagements at TU München, the Harvard Graduate School of Design, the Accademia di Architettura di Mendrisio and Yale University, as well as his participation in solo and group exhibitions, including at the Venice Biennale of Architecture, the Museo ICO in Madrid, the Architekturmuseum in Munich and the Philadelphia Museum of Art.

Prof. Dr. Kai A. Konrad is Director at the Max Planck Institute for Tax Law and Public Finance and a Scientific Member of the Max Planck Society. He was a Full Professor of Economics at the Freie Universität Berlin from 1994 to 2009, and from 2001 to 2009 he was a Director at the Wissenschaftszentrum Berlin für Sozialforschung (WZB). He is a member of the German National Academy of Sciences Leopoldina and of four other science academies. From 2007 to 2018 he was a Co-editor of the *Journal of Public Economics*. Since 1999 he has been a member of the Council of Scientific Advisors to the Federal Ministry of Finance and was the Chair from 2011 to 2014.

Prof. Dr. Stefan Korioth gained his doctorate in law in 1990 and completed his postdoctoral qualification in public and constitutional law. From 1996 to 2000 he was Professor of Public Law, Constitutional History, and Theory of Government at the University of Greifswald. In 2000 he accepted the Chair of Public and Ecclesiastical Law at Ludwig Maximilian University, Munich. His publications include

Integration un₁ Bun₁esstaat (1990), *Der Finanzausgleich zwischen Bun₁ un₁ Län₁ern* (1997), *Grun₁züge ₁es Staatskirchenrechts* (with B. Jean d'Heur, 2000), *Das Bun₁esverfassungsgericht* (with Klaus Schlaich, 12th edition, 2021), and *Staatsrecht I* (6th edition, 2022).

Prof. Dr. Jörn Leonhard is Chair of Western European History at the Albert Ludwig University of Freiburg, and an author. Having studied history, political science, and German philology in Heidelberg and Oxford, he received his Ph.D. in 1998 and completed his postdoctoral qualification at Heidelberg University in 2004. From 1998 to 2003 he was a Fellow and Tutor at Oxford University; Visiting Research Fellow at the Alexander von Humboldt Foundation in the German-American Center for Visiting Scholars in Washington, D.C. in 2001; Fellow of the Royal Historical Society London since 2002; and Senior Fellow at the Institute for Contemporary History of the Historisches Kolleg in Munich from 2016 to 2017. From 2007 to 2012 he was Director of the School of History at the Freiburg Institute for Advanced Studies (FRIAS) and in 2012/13 Visiting Professor at Harvard University. His research and publications have received multiple awards. His most recent English publication is *Pan₁ora's Box: A History of the First Worl₁*

War (2018). Jörn Leonhard has been full member of the Heidelberg Academy of Sciences and Humanities since 2015 and Honorary Fellow of Wadham College, Oxford University, since 2019.

Prof. Dr. Timo Meynhardt holds the Dr. Arend Oetker Chair of Business Psychology and Leadership at the HHL Leipzig Graduate School of Management. He is Managing Director of the Center for Leadership and Values in Society at the University of St. Gallen, where he obtained his doctorate and postdoctoral qualification in business administration. For several years, he was Practice Expert at McKinsey & Company. Timo Meynhardt's work focuses on public value management and leadership, combining psychology and business management in his research and teaching. He is co-developer of the Leipzig leadership model and co-publisher of the *Public Value Atlas* for Switzerland and Germany, which aims at making transparent the social benefits of companies and organizations (www. gemeinwohlatlas.de; www.gemeinwohl.ch). His Public Value Scorecard provides a management tool to measure and analyze the creation of public value. He is also Co-founder and Jury Member of the Public Value Awards for Startups.

Hans Ulrich Obrist (b. 1968, Zurich, Switzerland) is Artistic Director of the Serpentine in London and Senior Advisor at LUMA Arles. Prior to this, he was the Curator of the Musée d'Art Moderne de la Ville de Paris. Since his first show "World Soup (The Kitchen Show)" in 1991, he has curated more than 350 exhibitions. His recent shows include "IT'S URGENT" at LUMA Arles (2019–21) and "Enzo Mari" at Triennale Milano (2020). In 2011 Obrist received the CCS Bard Award for Curatorial Excellence, and in 2015 he was awarded the International Folkwang Prize, and most recently he was honored by the Appraisers Association of America with the 2018 Award for Excellence in the Arts. Obrist's recent publications include *Ways of Curating* (2015), *The Age of Earthquakes* (2015), *Lives of the Artists, Lives of Architects* (2015), *Mondialité* (2017), *Somewhere Totally Else* (2018), *The Athens Dialogues* (2018), *Maria Lassnig: Letters* (2020), *Entrevistas Brasileiras: Volume 2* (2020), *An Exhibition Always Hides Another Exhibition* (2019), *The Extreme Self: Age of You* (2021), and *140 Ideas for Planet Earth* (2021).

Prof. em. Dr. Christoph G. Paulus studied law at Munich, taking his doctorate in law in 1980. His post-doctoral qualification, gained in 1991, was in civil law, civil procedure, and Roman law, for which he was awarded the Medal of the University of Paris II. Between 1989 and 1990 he was a recipient of a Feodor Lynen Stipend from the Humboldt Foundation in Berkeley, from which he had earlier gained his LLM. From 1992 to 1994 he was Associate Professor at Augsburg, and from the summer semester 1994 he was at the Law Faculty of Humboldt University in Berlin, becoming Dean of the Faculty 2008–10. He is Consultant to the International Monetary Fund and the World Bank. Among other roles, he is a member of the International Insolvency Institute of the American College of Bankruptcy and the International Association for Procedural Law. From 2006 to 2010 he was advisor on insolvency law to the German delegation to UNCITRAL. He is on the editorial board of the Zeitschrift für Wirtschaftsrecht (ZIP), the Northern Annual Review of International Insolvency, and the International Insolvency Law Review.

Prof. Mathias Risse, Ph.D. is Berthold Beitz Professor in Human Rights, Global Affairs and Philosophy and Director of the Carr Center for Human Rights Policy at Harvard University. His work primarily addresses questions of global justice, ranging from human rights, inequality, taxation, trade and immigration to climate change, obligations to future generations and the future of technology, especially also the impact of artificial intelligence on a range of normative issues. He has also worked on questions in ethics, decision theory and 19th century German philosophy, especially Nietzsche. Risse is the author of *Global Political Philosophy* (2012), *On Global Justice* (2013), *On Trave Justice: A Philosophical Plea for a New Global Deal* (with Gabriel Wollner, 2019) and *On Justice: Philosophy, History, Founıations* (2020). Risse serves as Co-Director of Graduate Studies at the Edmond J Safra Center for Ethics as well as Director of the McCloy program, a fellowship program for German students. He is also affiliated with the Weatherhead Center for International Affairs.

Prof. Dr. Dr. h.c. Wolfgang Schön studied law and economics at the University of Bonn. He was Professor at the University of Bielefeld from 1992 to 1996, and from 1996 to 2002 at the University of Bonn. Since 2002 he has been Director and Scientific Member of the Max Planck Institute for Tax Law and Public Finance in Munich. He is Honorary Professor at Ludwig Maximilian University Munich; member of the Global Law Faculty, New York University; and International Research Fellow, University of Oxford Centre of Business Taxation. From 2008 to 2014 Prof. Schön was Vice-President of the Max Planck Society. Since 2014 he has been Vice-President of the German Research Foundation (DFG). He has published numerous works on German and European company law, competition law, and tax law.

Prof. Dr. Claudia Wiesner is Jean Monnet Chair and Professor for Political Science at Fulda University of Applied Sciences and Adjunct Professor in Political Science at Jyväskylä University. She leads several international research projects and networks and is Executive Director of the newly founded research institute Point Alpha e.V. In addition, she has been a Visiting Fellow at such institutions as the Center for European Studies at Harvard University, the Berlin Social Studies Centre, and the Robert Schuman Centre for Advanced Studies at the European University Institute (EUI). Her main research interests lie in the comparative study of democracy in the EU and its Member States, comparative research into policy innovations, and model projects and key concepts in political science. Recent publications include: *The European Central Bank between the Financial Crisis an￯ Populisms* (Palgrave Macmillan, with Corrado Macchiarelli, Mara Monti, and Sebastian Diessner), and *Rethinking Politicisation in Politics, Sociology an￯*

International Relations (Palgrave Macmillan, edited by Claudia Wiesner).

Prof. Jonathan Wolff, Ph.D. is the Alfred Landecker Professor of Values and Public Policy and Governing Body Fellow at Wolfson College. Jonathan was formerly Blavatnik Chair in Public Policy at the School, and before that Professor of Philosophy and Dean of Arts and Humanities at UCL. He is currently developing a new research program on revitalizing democracy and civil society, in accordance with the aims of the Alfred Landecker Professorship. His other current work largely concerns equality, disadvantage, social justice, and poverty, as well as applied topics such as public safety, disability, gambling, and the regulation of recreational drugs, which he has discussed in his books *Ethics and Public Policy: A Philosophical Inquiry* (Routledge, 2011) and *The Human Right to Health* (Norton, 2012). His most recent book is *An Introduction to Moral Philosophy* (Norton, 2018).

Earlier works include *Disadvantage* (OUP, 2007), with Avner de-Shalit; *An Introduction to Political Philosophy* (OUP, 1996, third edition 2016); *Why Read Marx Today?* (OUP, 2002); and *Robert Nozick* (Polity, 1991). He has had a long-standing interest in health and health promotion, including questions of justice in healthcare resource allocation, the social determinants of health, and incentives and health behavior. He has been a member of the Nuffield Council of Bioethics, the Academy of Medical Science working party on Drug Futures, the Gambling Review Body, the Homicide Review Group, an external member of the Board of Science of the British Medical Association, and a Trustee of GambleAware. He writes a regular column on higher education for *The Guardian*.

Podcast Conversations

The CONVOCO! podcasts on the topic of "Equality in an Unequal World" by Corinne M. Flick in conversation with:

#89: What is Status Anxiety, and How Do We Escape It?

Alain de Botton

#81: What Has Led to Today's Inequalities?

Prof. Oded Galor, Ph.D.

#80: Why Equality is about Dignity and Respect

Prof. Tim Crane, Ph.D.

#78: Why Justice needs both Equity and Equality

Dr. Georgia Dawson

#61: A World of Heightened Risk: Trends and Reasons for Optimism

Dr. Maha H. Aziz

#57: Do We Need a New Social Contract?

Baroness Minouche Shafik

#55: How the Discrimination of Women is Built into the Global Economy

Prof. Dr. Linda Scott

**HOW MUCH FREEDOM MUST WE FORGO
TO BE FREE?** *2022*

ISBN: 978-1-9163673-4-0

With contributions by: Bazon Brock, Tim Crane, Gabriel Felbermayr, Clemens Fuest, Birke Häcker, Martha Jungwirth, Bruno Kahl, Stefan Korioth, Jörn Leonhart, Rudolf Mellinghoff, Timo Meynhardt, Hans Ulrich Obrist, Philipp Pattberg, Herbert A. Reitsamer, Monika Schnitzer, Sven Simon, Claudia Wiesner, Peter Wittig, Hildegard Wortmann

**NEW GLOBAL ALLIANCES: INSTITUTIONS,
ALIGNMENTS AND LEGITIMACY IN THE
CONTEMPORARY WORLD** *2021*

ISBN: 978-1-9163673-2-6

With contributions by: Maha Hosain Aziz, Bazon Brock, Garrett Wallace Brown, Udo Di Fabio, Clemens Fuest, Eugénia C. Helt, Stefan Korioth, Jörn Leonhart, Rudolf Mellinghoff, Timo Meynhardt, Stefan Oschmann, Christoph G. Paulus, Gisbert Rühl, Wolfgang Schön, Sven Simon, Lothar H. Wieler

THE STANDING OF EUROPE IN THE NEW IMPERIAL WORLD ORDER *2020*

ISBN: 978-1-9163673-0-2

With contributions by: Fredrik Erixon, Gabriel Felbermayr, Birke Häcker, Matthias Karl, Parag Khanna, Kai A. Konrad, Stefan Korioth, Jörn Leonhard, Timo Meynhardt, Hans Ulrich Obrist with Edi Rama, Stefan Oschmann, Christoph G. Paulus, Rupprecht Podszun, Jörg Rocholl, Sven Simon, Yael Tamir, Roberto Viola, Claudia Wiesner

THE MULTIPLE FUTURES OF CAPITALISM *2019*

ISBN: 978-0-9931953-8-9

With contributions by: Lucio Baccaro, Jens Beckert, Bazon Brock, Corinne M. Flick, Sean Hagan, Kai A. Konrad, Stefan Korioth, Justin Yifu Lin, Rudolf Mellinghoff, Timo Meynhardt, Hans Ulrich Obrist with Adam Curtis, Stefan Oschmann, Christoph G. Paulus, Herbert A. Reitsamer, Albrecht Ritschl, Jörg Rocholl, Gisbert Rühl, Monika Schnitzer, Wolfgang Schön

THE COMMON GOOD IN THE 21ST CENTURY *2018*

ISBN: 978-0-9931953-6-5

AUTHORITY IN TRANSFORMATION *2017*

ISBN: 978-0-9931953-4-1

POWER AND ITS PARADOXES *2016*

ISBN: 978-0-9931953-2-7

TO DO OR NOT TO DO—INACTION AS A FORM OF ACTION *2015*

ISBN: 978-0-9931953-0-3

DEALING WITH DOWNTURNS: STRATEGIES IN UNCERTAIN TIMES *2014*

ISBN: 978-0-9572958-8-9

COLLECTIVE LAW-BREAKING—A THREAT TO LIBERTY *2013*

ISBN: 978-0-9572958-5-8

WHO OWNS THE WORLD'S KNOWLEDGE? *2012*

ISBN: 978-0-9572958-0-3

CAN'T PAY, WON'T PAY? SOVEREIGN DEBT AND THE CHALLENGE OF GROWTH IN EUROPE *2011*

ISBN: 978-0-9572958-3-4

www.ingramcontent.com/pod-product-compliance
Lightning Source LLC
Chambersburg PA
CBHW070759280326
41934CB00012B/2981